JOHN NETTLES'
JERSEY

A personal history
of the people &
places

BBC BOOKS

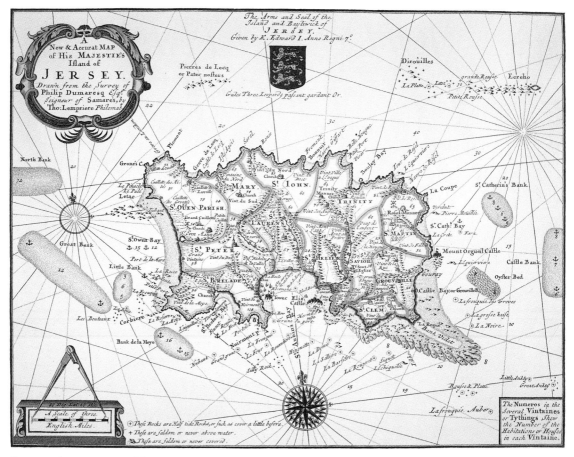

Seventeenth-century map of Jersey.

Published by BBC Books,
a division of BBC Enterprises Limited,
Woodlands, 80 Wood Lane, London W12 0TT
First published 1992
© John Nettles 1992
ISBN 0 563 36318 5
Specially commissioned photographs by David Ward
Set in 11/14pt Sabon by Butler & Tanner Ltd, Frome
Printed and bound in Great Britain by Butler & Tanner Ltd, Frome
Colour separations by Technik Ltd, Berkhamsted
Colour printing by Lawrence Allen Ltd, Weston-super-Mare
Jacket printed by Belmont Press Ltd, Northampton

CONTENTS

ACKNOWLEDGEMENTS

In writing this book I have had cause to be grateful to many people. Amongst many others I would like to thank Assistant Chief Officers Robert le Breton and Barry Simpson, Superintendent Martin le Brocq and, particularly, P C Robert Aldgate for their invaluable assistance in the telling of the Newalls' story. My especial thanks in this same connection to Chief Superintendent John Saunders and to Maureen and David Ellam. Sometime in the near future I would like to write the last chapter of this tragic story.

My thanks also to Mary Phillips for letting me share a little of her encyclopaedic knowledge of murder in Jersey.

Thanks to Anthony le Gallais for allowing me so much of his time, and access to his private collection of Lillie Langtry memorabilia.

To Mrs Resch, Mr McGarry, Mr le Brun and many other Jersey folk for kindly sharing their memories of the Occupation with me.

Last, but by no means least, many thanks to the staff of *La Société Jersiaise*, especially Catherine Buddin, Lucy Marder and Jonathan Carter.

This list would by no means be complete without mention of Tessa Coleman who gave more than generously of her time in the creation of what follows.

PREFACE

This book is the result of a kind of love affair I have had with Jersey since 1980, and which I think will last for a long time yet. I wanted to find out all I possibly could about her people and her past – and a fascinating study it turned out to be. The island's history teems with marvellous characters and events, many more than one has a right to expect in an area only 14.5 km by 8 km (nine miles by five). In the course of researching for this book, I have come across amazing stories involving extraordinary people in often very strange adventures. I believe I have only just scratched the surface.

But it has been a truly enjoyable experience to learn of those forces and personalities, anything but obscure, which have made this island what it is, and to make the acquaintance of that tremendous character Sir George Carteret, the tragic and forlorn Philippe d'Auvergne and the fabulous Lillie Langtry. It was not quite so pleasant, it must be said, to research the awful and bloody case of the murdered Newalls, but I thank all those people who gave unstintingly of their time and professional expertise to help me put together a picture of that stormracked week in October 1987. I have to add, too, that I have received great support and help from the staff of *La Société Jersiaise*, who allowed me access to their extensive records and to their art treasures. Indeed, everyone I asked to help me responded splendidly; from Lieutenant-Governor Sir John Sutton to my friendly garage-owner, who wishes to remain anonymous, no one has refused to help me. I am exceedingly grateful, therefore, to the islanders.

It has been said, with some truth, that the television series *Bergerac* portrays the island as a millionaires' paradise, full of criminals and shady characters with almost a crime a minute. It does, indeed, so picture Jersey, but everyone of sense understands that this is television fiction, about as believable as the eponymous hero's unerring ability to solve a crime a week in under 60 minutes. However, not everyone may understand the real nature of this island, its history and where the true genius of its people lies. I hope this book will shed some light on these subjects. It is my way of saying 'thank you' to Jersey, for ten most enjoyable years.

Panoramic view across St Aubin's Bay, the 'gateway to Jersey' (1875). It is very different now because of new roads, huge land-reclamation projects and the construction of new harbours in St Helier.

INTRODUCTION

Some sunlit morning, stand by the old granite church in St Brelade and look, if you will, south-eastward beyond the harbour wall, far across the fine sweep of the bay, to the vaulting cliffs by the Ouaisne slip. There is the great cave called La Cotte, where the earliest Jerseyman lived a quarter of a million years ago. Assiduous archaeologists have found the mortal remains of Neanderthal man, and those of his prey the rhinoceros and the great mammoth, held fast in the rocky fissures. Simply, efficiently, man the hunter would drive these huge beasts before him, over and down the cliff face to certain death. The animals were butchered and eaten there on the rocky beaches below. This view across the bay to La Cotte de St Brelade must be little changed by time or man. Turn your gaze landward to the left a little, and judge for yourself the vision of those who have but lately inherited this most beautiful of islands.

Much indeed has changed, but what is truly remarkable is how much remains to be seen, touched, enjoyed and wondered at.

The curious traveller may climb to the extraordinary and lovingly restored passage grave at La Hougue Bie, built on the high lands in the south-east of the island that look clear across the royal bay of Grouville to the coast of France. Five thousand years old, the grave was built of huge stone slabs hauled the three long miles from St Helier or dragged with rawhide cables up the steep hills of Anne Port Bay or Mont Mado. The largest slab weighs 20 tonnes. Seven hundred tonnes of rock were moved to make this grave. It is one of the finest sites in Western Europe, impressive testimony to the technical skills and, more important, the spirituality of so-called primitive men whose life expectancy was exactly half that of ours. You will find not just this one reminder of our furthest past but many, scattered with great largesse about every corner of Jersey.

For instance, on the other side of the island, north of L'Etacq, a great granite rock soars high into the sky, joined to the land by a little valley carpeted with grass and gorse. This is Le Pinacle, an eerie, dramatic place thought to have been used by successive generations of settlers for the solemn observances of religious rituals. In the light of the rising or setting sun, the shadows on Le Pinacle seem to form themselves into the likeness of a face: great depressions in the stone

for the eyes, the huge mouth carved out below. If we can see it now, perhaps our forebears also could and, just maybe, they invested the phenomenon with a spiritual significance. This may be conjecture, but it is certain that from the landward heights the outline of an exceedingly rare Roman kind of shrine can be clearly seen on the floor of the valley behind the great rock. The climb down is steep. The experience of standing within the holy place is inexpressible.

Left and below: The neolithic passage grave at La Hougue Bie, lovingly restored by *La Société Jersiaise*. Our forebears manhandled the huge stone slabs for many miles to create this magnificent tomb, the last resting-place for sixteen people. La Hougue Bie is one of the richest archaeological sites in western Europe.

Overleaf: Le Pinacle, one of the most mysterious, imposing and beautiful places on the island. There is a ruined temple at its foot and important neolithic remains a little to its north.

Not that Jersey has always been careful of her heritage. In 1785, while excavating on Town Hill, or Mont de Ville, to make a parade ground for the St Helier militia, another very fine example of a passage grave was uncovered. It had a central circular chamber formed of 30 huge stone slabs up to 2.5 metres ($8\frac{1}{2}$ feet) high joined by massive capstones some 4.5 metres (15 feet) long. In 1787, Jerseymen with more ambition to please their benevolent governor, Henry Conway, than care to preserve an important monument for the island, gave the entire edifice over to him. More a modern man of battle than antiquarian enthusiast, he at first thought to refuse the proffered gift; but his cousin, Horace Walpole, persuaded him to accept the monument. Conway transported it, stone by stone, and re-erected it in a new and somewhat incongruous setting: the pleasantly bland countryside of Henley-on-Thames in England where it looked, as Walpole remarked, like a little Stonehenge and 'very high priestly'.

It would be difficult, indeed impossible, to bring the stones back and replace them on their former site and in their former splendour. Since 1814, Town Hill has boasted a very splendid fort – Fort Regent – on its summit. This brilliantly designed fortification was the work of Major John Hambly Humfrey and, by all accounts, is one of the best of its kind in the world. Unfortunately, it was completed in the very year when the threat it was meant to counter disappeared: Napoleon was exiled to Elba.

It has never figured in any military engagement, unless you can count the Germans firing off a few rounds at marauding Allied aircraft during the Second World War. The Jersey Government bought Fort Regent in 1958 and it is now a leisure centre of some pretension, and subject to much criticism.

Whatever its present demerits, it is none the less a marvellously fine vantage point from which to look out over the panorama of St Aubin's Bay. Most of Jersey's history is in this spectacle. There is Elizabeth Castle, built on The Islet to replace the Old Castle at Gorey and beyond it, a little further out to sea, there is the little oratory built on Hermitage Rock, where St Helier or St Helius, who gave his name to the town of St Helier, lived. He was a holy man, an ascetic Christian of the sixth century, who came to Jersey from Gaul and lived in a hollow carved in the rock of The Islet. He fasted long and suffered much. The story is told that, when he was very weak from self-denial, St Marculf, a friend of many years, came to visit him. At this time a fleet of pirates from Orkney was spied bearing down upon the island. St Helier and St Marculf resolved to offer no armed resistance to the raiders, but instead prayed mightily to God that he might deliver them from their enemies. God was apparently not deaf to their pleas, for legend has it that the buccaneers suddenly quarrelled among themselves and killed each other; out of 3000 of them, not one remained alive.

Poor St Helier was not so fortunate as to be within hailing distance of the Almighty when, some 12 years later, another group of brigands – we don't know whether they were from North Africa or from Scandinavia – descended upon the island. They found the saint weak and in hiding and promptly beheaded him, allowing him no shriving time. The oratory built in the twelfth century remains a perpetual memorial to the man who gave his name to the capital of Jersey.

Then there is Elizabeth Castle itself, spread out below. During the seventeenth century, it was witness to the most colourful, bloody and exciting period of Jersey's history. This was the time when that greatest of great Jerseymen, Sir George Carteret, walked the battlements to view the tiny homeland he kept in perilous, but ultimately profitable, trust for the future Charles II of England. For a long time the history of Jersey was the history of George Carteret. His manor house at St Ouen is still there, in the benign care of Philip Malet de Carteret. Here, if you are so minded, you may see the king's letter to Sir George, which includes the heartfelt postscript: 'Carteret, I will add to you under my own hand. That I can never forget the good services you have done to my father and to me and if God bless me you shall find I do remember them to the advantage to you and yours and for this you have the word of your ever loving friend Charles R.'

Away across those sands where the pride of Jersey's manhood paraded for the young King Charles during his sojourn on the island in 1649, lies St Aubin, at one time the main port for the island. Here, it is rumoured, many Huguenots fleeing from religious persecution in France were lured into lodging-houses only to be robbed and have their throats cut by murderously entrepreneurial Jerseymen.

A better sort of Jerseyman altogether lived hard by St Aubin during the last century, in the shape of Sir John Le Couteur, aide-de-camp to William IV and then to Queen Victoria, Fellow of the Royal Society, Vicomte (senior judicial officer) of Jersey and creator of the

Jersey cow. He it was who, on the occasion of the royal visit in the summer of 1846, accompanied Her Majesty and the Prince Albert about the streets of St Helier and then to Gorey and to Mont Orgueil Castle, which has mercifully been saved intact for us and for posterity by no less a person than Sir Walter Raleigh, Governor of Jersey between 1600 and 1603.

Sir Walter admitted that the castle was overlooked by a hill to the west and so was very difficult to defend, but nevertheless, in a memorandum to Elizabeth I, advised that it was 'a stately fort of great capacity, so until I know further Her Majesty's pleasure, I have left at my own charge some men in it and if a small matter may defend it, it were a pity to cast it down having cost Her Majesty's father, brother and sister without her own charge 20 000 marks in erecting.' Mont Orgueil remained, and remains, as do those massive constructions built by the Germans during the Second World War.

Everywhere on the island there is evidence of the onerous German Occupation, which lasted from 1940 to 1945. Noirmont Point – from Fort Regent it can be seen reaching out into the Channel – has no less than nineteen military installations built into and upon it: observation towers, command bunkers, gun emplacements and communication centres. Every exposed beach in Jersey is guarded by massive bunkers. Unsightly fire towers are built on top of the ancient castles, and miles of sea defences, using thousands of tons of concrete, were erected, largely by the efforts of unfortunate and cruelly mistreated workers shipped in from all over Europe and, mainly, Russia by the Todt organisation. They also built the infamous underground hospital in St Peter's Valley, where, as Dr John Lewis recounts in *A Doctor's Occupation,* towards the end of the war operations were performed without anaesthetic on wretched German soldiers hurt and maimed during the Allied landings in France.

Perhaps one day, sometime in the future when memories of those cruel years have finally faded to nothing, we will regard the Nazis' handiwork with the disinterested curiosity with which we now view earlier military relics from the Napoleonic Wars; the barracks, the old forts and the round Martello Towers. But a lot of grass will have to grow before that time comes.

Below the formidable granite ramparts of Fort Regent lies St Helier, sprawled higgledy-piggledy and possessed of an impenetrable one-way system and many office blocks eloquent of Jersey's status as a favoured offshore banking centre. It is an eclectic mixture of

Above: The Jersey cow. It looks delicate but it is a hardy beast, created by Sir John Le Couteur in the last century.

Right: The gilded statue of George II in the Royal Square, St Helier. For many years it was thought to be the figure of a Roman emperor rescued from a wrecked ship.

architectural styles and, come high summer, thousands of holiday-makers from mainland Britain, shiny with suntan oil, crowd in and around the gift and souvenir shops that proliferate everywhere. It is by no means a uniformly pretty place. Indeed, C. E. B. Brett, in his 1977 survey of buildings of the town and parish of St Helier, remarked truthfully, if shrewishly, that, 'The States of Jersey Building, the political heart of this island, looks like nothing so much as a great warship run unaccountably aground alongside the Royal Square.' There are, it is true, some very pleasant crescents and, here and there, some quite fine Regency-style town houses and a couple of very splendid churches. But generally speaking the shops and houses and office blocks are of a style that may be described as functional – if you want to be kind.

At night-time St Helier offers little but booze and cheap entertainment in the form of unlovely discothèques and the performance of low farce. That is to say, it offers nothing that is distinctively Jersey. You could be anywhere in the United Kingdom. It is the end of the relatively short process of making the island more English and less Norman French that began at the end of the Napoleonic Wars. At that time, many ex-military men and their dependants came to the island, pensioned off from those wars, to set up home in the pleasant air of Jersey. The population grew from 28 600 in 1821 to about 57 000 in 1851. Gradually but surely, the old distinctive ways and customs of the island began to change. The number of people speaking the native patois, Norman French, began inexorably to decline to its present number of about 5000 in a population of about 85 000. Perhaps even more significantly, the proportion of native-born Jersey folk began to diminish as well. According to the 1990 census, less than 50 per cent of the present inhabitants are native islanders.

This process of determined Anglicisation is now almost complete; let the advertisements for tourism say what they will, almost the only French aspect of the island is its proximity to Normandy. Everything else is clearly, and provincially, British. You have to look hard to find old and beautiful granite houses built in the vernacular style, and even harder to discover that idiosyncratic and particular insular spirit that sets Jersey apart from everywhere else in the Western world.

Through the years that spirit has declared itself most eloquently through the States Assembly, the island parliament. This parliament is made up of the queen's representative, the lieutenant-governor, who has no voice in its proceedings, being largely decorative; the bailiff, who is not decorative and who presides over the chamber and may, and often does, have a very loud voice indeed; twelve elected senators and twelve elected constables (or *connétables*), one from each of the twelve parishes; and twenty-nine deputies. These are the people who decide what is best for the island and what policies to pursue to achieve that goal.

The executive and legislative machinery has worked very well in the past. It will need to work even better in the future, for Jersey has some formidable problems to face. For instance, how many and what sort of people should be allowed in? And, once here, how should they be treated – like full members of the community or like second-class citizens deprived of certain rights regarded as natural and inalienable in other Western countries? How much and what sort of land development should the States allow? As much as the growing financial and tourism industries want? Or as little as the conservationist lobby thinks compatible with preserving all that makes this island beautiful?

These are serious issues and the debate is consequently and expectedly furious. There is a Jersey Rights Association intent on gaining fundamental rights for long-term immigrant workers in the so-called J category (someone 'essentially employed'). There is a conservationist lobby intent on scotching at birth seriously considered plans such as the one to build an airstrip in the middle of the Channel between the east of the island and France, and so destroy one of the most beautiful waterways of Europe. Further, what will happen when Jersey becomes an even closer member of the European Community? Will the financial industry suffer, and is there anything that can be done to preserve it as the major single factor in a burgeoning island economy?

Troubled times indeed for the States members, but it is not the first time the guardians of Jersey's welfare have endured dark nights of the soul. Fortunately, during most of these periods, a Carteret (the Civil War) or a Coutanche (the Second World War) has always been at hand to guide, cajole or bully the islanders, sometimes against all odds, in the direction that suits them best. What follows is an account of some of those colourful times and even more colourful characters in Jersey's history. Stories of heroism and sacrifice, vice, stupidity, cruelty, torture, mystery and romance. Stories, too, of Jersey folk whose fabulous careers took them to the corners of the world, but who had their origins in Jersey – an island Sir James Brodie once called, 'the El Dorado of Earth'.

An unusually quiet spot on the eastern coast. It looks across the narrow Channel towards France, and across the jagged rocks that served for centuries as the island's sure defence.

1

BEGINNINGS

Certain mainland politicians perennially moan that Jersey enjoys unfair advantages over the rest of the United Kingdom. Why should the islanders be taxed only 20p in the pound? Why should there be no death duties? And, above all, why should there be no capital gains tax? A millionaire of the kind often seen in a certain television programme invests his money, sits back and rakes in a handsome profit: a man with, say, £7 million on deposit can expect an income from the interest of £2000 a day, absolutely tax-free. This state of affairs is intolerable, they cry, and should be brought to an end forthwith. Jersey should be governed by the same laws, and observe the same rules, as the rest of the United Kingdom.

The briefest look at the history and constitution of the island would help to rearrange their ideas. Jersey is not, and never has been, a part of the United Kingdom in the sense that, say, Wales is. The islanders have no representation in, nor duty of obligation to, the Parliament in Westminster. Jersey, in the historian Philip Falle's pithy phrase, is a 'Peculiar of the Crown not a parcel of the Realm of England', in that it has its own parliament, the States, and its ultimate ruler is the monarch in Privy Council not the British Parliament. In practice most, if not all, legislation originates on the island; if it does happen to originate in Britain in the Council, the States are closely consulted. If, however, there is a disagreement between the wishes of the Privy Council and the island parliament, a 'Peremptory order may constitutionally be issued' (A. J. Eagleston) by the Privy Council which the island rulers are bound to implement with no further appeal allowed. In practice disagreements are usually resolved long before the issue of such an order becomes necessary, and the island enjoys a considerable degree of autonomy that has been jealously guarded down the centuries. It would be a hazardous undertaking to try and separate the Jerseyman from his freedoms.

It all began in 1066 when William the Conqueror, after the defeat of Harold, became King of England as well as Duke of Normandy of which Jersey formed part. This did not significantly alter the political affiliation of Jersey. It remained a part of Normandy with Norman laws, and allegiances to a Norman duke who also happened to be king in another place. In 1204, when John, King of England and Duke of Normandy, lost Normandy to France, the islands remained under the control of the King of England.

The history of Jersey as a 'Peculiar of the Crown' dates from this time. Its particular rights and freedoms, reflecting its unique relation to the English monarch, have been confirmed by every successive sovereign down to modern times.

Jersey became the outpost of England, facing an ever-hostile France. The history of the next seven centuries is largely the history of conflict, with invading forces coming out of Normandy and causing great suffering among the islanders, as in the fourteenth century when the awesome, savage and very clever Bertrand du Guesclin, Constable of France, came roaring in with his army, forced the great castle of Mont Orgueil to surrender and held the entire island in his thrall for seven long and terrible years. He was a cruel and vicious lord, not averse to torture and burning to get his way. The islanders must have been more than a little pleased when he died in 1380.

His invasion set the pattern of island life for centuries to come. It was one of constant vigilance and warlike preparation, the keeping of everlasting watch and ward all about the coasts for invaders who appeared with awful regularity on their missions of conquest and pillage. Before the German Occupation the last, briefly successful, attempt to invade the island came in 1781.

Jersey pirates, or privateers as they were more respectably known, were a perpetual threat and nuisance to French shipping. Ever since the seventeenth century, Jersey seamen had been notorious for their piracy and their depredations. During the Seven Years War (1756–63), when England and Prussia allied against France and Austria, the English used them as an arm of the navy to attack France – and attack they did, with enthusiasm. They brought scores of French prizes to St Aubin and St Helier, to be auctioned off and the spoils divided. These activities brought a vengeful invasion force to the island in 1781, commanded by a brave, audacious and resourceful mercenary: Baron de Rullecourt. His attempt on Jersey was delayed by inclement weather, but he finally landed his troops at La Rocque where they were least expected; somehow, and some people say with the help of a traitorous Jerseyman called Journeaux, Rullecourt managed to

Overleaf: Moonscape Beach, so called for its unearthly appearance at low water. Baron de Rullecourt had to navigate these shark-toothed rocks and sandbanks to invade Jersey in 1781.

21

The brave and audacious Rullecourt lands at La Rocque. He might have saved himself the trouble and, as it turned out, his life. A public convenience now stands on the spot.

navigate his vessels through the treacherous, jagged shark-toothed rocks that protect Jersey's eastern seaboard. He landed a few of his soldiers from his seven boats before the tide turned. The men of the Jersey militia, who should have been on guard that night, were too busy celebrating Twelfth Night and drinking cider to notice what was happening. Rullecourt's men overpowered them and advanced quickly under cover of darkness to St Helier. There they surprised the Lieutenant-Governor of Jersey, Moyse Corbet, in his nightshirt and took him prisoner. Corbet surrendered the island to the bold Frenchman, believing him to have 10 000 men at his back: he had only 600 soldiers.

The lieutenant-governor sent out orders to the military commanders in every parish that they should surrender. They declined to do so. In particular, young Major Francis Peirson, in command of the 95th Foot in St Peter, declined. Swearing that he and his men would never surrender, he marched towards St Helier, joining a force of equally determined Scots just outside the town. Peirson sent the Scots to occupy Town Hill, a fine vantage-point overlooking St Helier, while he himself marched to the Royal Square where the French troops were drawn up. He split his force into two and attacked the French simultaneously from the north of the square, along what is now the King Street Precinct, and from the west along Library Place. The soldiers on Town Hill unleashed a murderous fire on the French position. Ferociously attacked from these three sides, Rullecourt's men gave up in a matter of minutes. The battle of Jersey was over almost before it had begun. Tragically, the youthful Major Peirson was killed in the action, as was his adversary Baron de Rullecourt. You will find monuments to both men in St Helier town church. Major Peirson's grave is by the chancel step. The battle of Jersey is commemorated in a fine painting by John Singleton Copley, a copy of which can be found in almost every house in Jersey.

Plus ça change. Jerseymen living in Elizabeth I's reign had had equal cause to fear attacks from France, particularly as the island had turned away from Catholicism and had become Protestant. In 1580, the Bishop of Coutances, in league with Henry III of France, tried to mount an attack on the island to restore it to the pope. Mercifully, the military invasion never came. However, there was another kind of invasion at this time, by Huguenot refugees cruelly driven from their own country by the Edict of San Maur and later by the bloody Massacre of St Bartholomew's Day. The Huguenots flocked in their hundreds to Jersey, intensifying its nonconformist character. The island was not loved in France by king or bishop and it was therefore necessary to make defences doubly sure.

As early as 1540 it had been realised that Mont Orgueil was out of date. It belonged to an older, outmoded form of medieval warfare. Modifications in the shape of new walls and battlements were carried out, but it was clear that the castle could no longer continue to be the centre of the island's defensive system. Another and better site had to be found for another and better castle. The site was The Islet of St Helier. The castle was Fort Isabella Bellissima, or Elizabeth Castle as it became known. Paul Ivy was the renowned engineer entrusted with its construction. Her Majesty Queen Elizabeth I graciously donated £500 towards the cost and the islanders bore the rest. They were taxed according to their means. Further, and more curiously, an Order in Council of 1551 decreed that each church in each parish should sell all but one of its bells and that the proceeds should go towards the construction of the castle and of the fort at St Aubin, which was seen as a necessary adjunct to the defensive capability of the castle. Between the two fortifications a line of guns could prevent all access along the whole length of St Aubin's Bay, the gateway to Jersey. Lose St Aubin's Fort and you open that gate to the invader, as the great Sir George Carteret discovered to his cost, a little later on.

A beautiful evocation of Elizabeth Castle at low water as it was in 1878, before the modern harbours were built.

2

A CREATURE OF THE KING

Sir George Carteret

(1610–80)

The de Carterets were the most powerful family in Jersey and, more than any other at this time, shaped the destiny of the island. Sir George's uncle, Sir Philippe, Seigneur of St Ouen, became Bailiff and Lieutenant-Governor of Jersey during the early part of the seventeenth century. By 1641, when England was on the brink of Civil War, he had ruled the island in a lordly, his detractors would call it a dictatorial, fashion for 15 years. His habit of appointing his supporters and members of his family to positions of high authority inevitably created envy and dislike among certain of the island community. When the conflict between the king and Parliament arose his opponents, animated as much by personal animosity as by political or religious conviction, saw their chance to topple him from power. They declared for Parliament. Sir Philippe, of course, declared for the king. So began a deadly struggle for the island that was to last for a whole decade. It is a most thrilling and extraordinary time, and brings on to the stage one of the greatest players in Jersey's dramatic history: Sir George Carteret.

George de Carteret was born in 1610. His parents were Elie and Elizabeth. His father was a younger son of the de Carteret family and therefore had little hope of great advancement. He had a small house at St Helier, and there little George lived happily with his brothers and sisters for 9 years. Elie then bought a small farm on Mont des Vignes in the parish of St Peter, to this day one of the most unspoilt and beautiful areas of the island. George spoke the local patois. He also spoke English, but with that strange accent that sounds a little like South African.

Sir George went to a local school, but learned little of the Greek and Latin on offer there. His real desire was to be a sailor in the fishing boats that voyaged westward from St Aubin to fish for cod in the freezing Newfoundland seas. He had his wish and was probably a seasoned sailor by the time he was sixteen, learning quickly how to sail, steer and navigate beneath the stars across the Atlantic waters. It was a complete apprenticeship in seamanship that was to stand him in good stead in later years.

His uncle, Sir Philippe de Carteret, now a great man in island life and a frequent visitor to London, managed to get young George a commission in the Royal Navy as a lieutenant aboard the *Garland*. It was a tiny ship, but what matter – his illustrious career had begun.

It was an exciting life. He sailed under that fine old seadog Admiral Sir John Penington, who was not content just to employ George's skills as a seaman, but put him ashore in France as a spy to find out the strength and state of preparation of the French fleet. At great risk to himself, but served well by his perfect command of French, George travelled to all the Normandy ports and gathered vital information for the Admiralty.

By way of reward, he was made captain of his first ship, the *Eighth Whelp*. After that he was given command of the thirty-gun *Happy Entrance* and of a fleet of six ships with which to patrol the strait of Dover.

The first great test of his abilities came in 1637, when he was ordered to sail against pirates working out of Sallee on the west coast of Africa. These men, devoutly Islam, harassed shipping in the English Channel unmercifully. They posed no small threat. Scores of ships and their crews were captured, millions of pounds were lost. At the time of Carteret's raid, over a thousand sailors and scores of women and children were held captive in Sallee.

George conducted a brilliant and audacious operation. Under cover of night, he rowed small boats right into Sallee harbour and fired many of the pirate ships. He made an alliance with the ruler of a neighbouring town and from there bombarded the buccaneers, who eventually surrendered. It was a triumph and George, as he was ever to do, reaped a rich reward. In 1638, he received from Charles I a patent giving him the office of Bailiff of Jersey after Sir Philippe de Carteret and Elie de Carteret. In 1640, Elie died and George was directly in line to succeed to the office of bailiff. His prospects were improving daily.

His private life was also developing well. In the year that his father died he married his cousin Elizabeth de Carteret, Sir Philippe's

Overleaf: An excellent example of true vernacular Jersey architecture, on the Mont des Vignes in the west of the island. This is the area where Sir George Carteret spent his early and formative years.

daughter. Their courtship was passionate; he wrote many times a week to her wherever he was. The marriage was long and loving; he was as devoted a husband and father as he was a servant of the king.

He called himself plain George Carteret, not de Carteret – he had dispensed with the 'de' when he joined the Royal Navy, for fear of being mistaken for a Frenchman. He was ever a passionate royalist, a creature of the king. More interestingly, he made the king a creature of George Carteret. 'By God, I will have almost brought it to that pass that the King shall not be able to whip a cat but that I mean to be at the tail of it,' he said. And, indeed, it seemed to many, particularly in his later years, that he walked the land with the king in his pocket, crown and all.

THE CIVIL WAR

In 1641, on the eve of the Civil War, George was at sea serving under his old friend Admiral Penington. However, he was looking seriously for a shore job and managed to be appointed Comptroller of the Royal Navy. It was not to last long.

In these desperate times, control of that mighty instrument of war, the navy, was vital. Robert Rich, Earl of Warwick, a staunch parliamentarian, was appointed Lord High Admiral, much to the chagrin of Charles I, who had desired his own man, Penington, to have the job. The parliamentarians then offered the post of Vice-admiral to George Carteret, who at that time was not thought to be particularly of one political persuasion or the other. George took it upon himself to enquire what the king wished in this regard. Charles told him to refuse the offer, which he did. This was, as that great seventeenth-century historian Sir Edward Hyde, later Earl of Clarendon, avers, an undoubted mistake. It is certain that Carteret's reputation was so great in the navy that he might have secured the loyalty and service of at least a substantial part of it for the king. This factor might just have changed the outcome of the internecine struggle.

As it was, George sent his pregnant wife Elizabeth back to Jersey away from seething murderous London, and then threw in his lot wholeheartedly with the royalist cause. Charles never had a better servant. George went to St Malo in Brittany and the king's party in Cornwall shipped cargoes of tin to him. Carteret sold the tin and, with the proceeds, purchased powder and munitions to send back into Cornwall, and in particular to Pendennis Castle. This was one of the very last of Charles' castles to surrender, largely because Carteret provided for it so very well. George's wife, with their new baby son Philip, came to St Malo to be with him, and he and his little family remained on French soil for 11 months.

Meanwhile, in Jersey, life was becoming dangerous for the royalists. Elizabeth Carteret's father, old Sir Philippe de Carteret, was loyal to the king, but he was much exercised to keep his little domain out of the civil conflagration on the mainland. He argued, with admirable constitutional cogency, that as Jersey owed allegiance only to the king and his Privy Council and not to Parliament, dissension between king and Parliament was a matter between the two warring factions alone. Jersey was not obliged to be involved. In the event, of course, it proved impossible to keep the island neutral and out of the Civil War. Sir Philippe himself was instrumental in bringing it into the conflict. He used his own vessels sailing from Jersey to ship supplies, bought in France by George, to Cornwall. Parliament retaliated by ordering his arrest. Puritan Jersey, disliking the whiff of popery about the king, and Sir Philippe even more, declared for Parliament. Sir Philippe retreated to Elizabeth Castle and his mother and his wife went to Mont Orgueil Castle. Both castles were besieged, but were consistently and adequately supplied by George Carteret from St Malo.

Below: Elizabeth Castle in 1650. It was the last royalist stronghold during the Civil War, defended by the doughty Sir George Carteret, possibly the greatest Jerseyman who ever lived.

Overleaf: Elizabeth Castle today, seen from Fort Charles.

A committee was set up in Jersey to prosecute the will of Parliament. It included among others David Bandinel, Dean of Jersey, and his son Jacques, rector of St Mary's, Michael Lempriere, M. D'Assigny and Abraham Herault. This committee complained bitterly to Parliament about Sir Philippe's practice of placing members of his own family in high office and other abuses of privilege. The allegations may or may not have been true, but it is clear from Jean Chevalier's contemporary diary that the committee, and Dean Bandinel in particular, treated Sir Philippe, his wife and his mother, not to mention his daughters, very cruelly indeed.

In 1643, Sir Philippe was old and he was dying. He asked for a minister from St Ouen to come and administer the last rites to him. The committee unfeelingly and peremptorily refused his request. His mother, more than 80 years old, then sought out members of the committee, Dean Bandinel and M. D'Assigny to ask for leave to enter the castle to comfort her dying son. She offered 20 ecus to the poor in return for being allowed to do so. The committee rejected this request. As Chevalier remarks, it was 'a lamentable thing for a mother to be unable to see her child, a wife her husband and sisters their brother, on his death bed.' Sir Philippe's mother sent a young girl to Elizabeth Castle with a book it was hoped would comfort him in his extremity. She was stopped on her journey by the committee members and the book was taken from her.

Three days after this, the committee sent a man into the castle to see if Sir Philippe were really ill. This agent confirmed that Sir Philippe was indeed sick, even dying, and that he begged the committee to let him have a last view of his wife before he passed away. The committee tardily agreed. Sir Philippe's wife and mother were allowed across the causeway. They were accompanied by his two daughters but one of them, Judy, was refused permission to enter the castle. She fainted and fell from her horse and was led back to St Helier. Eventually, the committee men allowed her to see her dying father when they heard he was crying out for her. They also let a minister across to administer the last rites, but not the man Sir Philippe had specifically requested.

It was a shabby episode in the island's history, and has been recounted at such length because it goes a good way to explaining George Carteret's harsh, unforgiving and rather ruthless treatment of those committee men when he gained power. He hunted them assiduously, as far as death itself – and he was not long in coming.

On Sir Philippe's death Charles I, from his beleaguered court at

Oxford, confirmed George Carteret in the office of Bailiff of Jersey. George bided his time. On the island, supporters of Parliament, the so-called well-affected party, seemed to be decreasing in number. The ordinary folk of Jersey were tired of keeping watch and ward continuously around the coast and besieging castles. They wished to return to their farms and a normal life. The new parliamentarian lieutenant-governor, Major Leonard Michael Lydcott, Michael Lempriere, the well-affected bailiff, and the committee men saw their support diminish everywhere on the island. Lydcott had been mis-informed about the degree of support for the parliamentary cause and had brought no soldiers with him. When the locally raised troops began to disband themselves he was left with no power whatsoever. The castles, however, remained impregnable.

Carteret's men struck. He himself landed at Mont Orgueil Castle on 18 November 1643 and on Tuesday 21 November royalists seized St Aubin's Fort after telling the Elizabeth Castle garrison what they were about to do. It was a surprisingly easy action: Carteret's men, with weapons concealed beneath their clothing, gradually insinuated themselves into the fort in small groups of two, three or four, seem-ingly intent only on gossiping with the garrison about the course of the war. When they were gathered in sufficient numbers, they overpowered the resident soldiers who, as our informed diarist Jean Chevalier tells us, 'Allowed themselves to be taken like poltroons.' On a prearranged signal a force was despatched from Elizabeth Castle to assist in occupying the fort. Other men went off to look for the commander of the tower – the unfortunate Lieutenant Brand. He was

Right: Mont Orgueil at Gorey. It was the island's major fortress until it was superseded by Elizabeth Castle.

Overleaf: Mont Orgueil Castle as it is today. Sir Walter Raleigh prevented its destruction at the end of the sixteenth century.

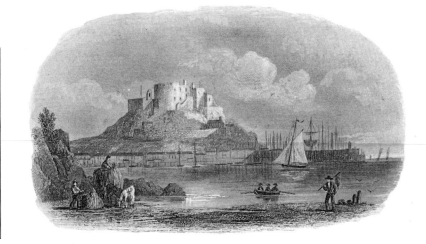

relaxing with a glass of wine and enjoying dinner with friends. Discretion being the better part of valour, he laid by his sword and surrendered without a fuss.

The capture of St Aubin's Fort was a signal for most of the important parliamentary men to flee. Lieutenant-Governor Lydcott, his wife, father and mother-in-law went first in a small, fast boat – a patache, kept hard by for such an eventuality. They were followed in short order by most of the committee men and their supporters. Those who remained were given short shrift.

By 22 November, Carteret was master of the island. He marched into St Helier, but there were no welcoming crowds: only deserted streets with just a few sobbing women to witness the procession. Perhaps, through their blurred vision, the sight of yet another Carteret riding triumphantly to power and dominion on the island looked like nothing more than a return to ways old and not much loved. Carteret was to remain lieutenant-governor for 8 years.

He certainly wasted no time. He compelled oaths of fealty from all the fearful populace. He summoned the States, the island parliament. This was his means to legality, although it was his poodle and would do exactly what he wished. He imprisoned those parliamentarians who had not had the foresight to escape, including the Dean of Jersey and his son Jacques, and confiscated their property – of which there was a great amount. Years later we find him still having trees cut down on the estate of Abraham Herault, who had fled the island on Sir George's advent, to help construct fortifications at Elizabeth Castle. It was a systematic purge of all elements in the island society which could be thought of as being remotely parliamentarian and against Sir George Carteret. He obtained a Commission from the king – Oyer et terminer – that empowered him to try matters of treason and lèse-majesté and to impose the death penalty on anyone judged guilty of such crimes. Since most of those who could be accused of treason had fled along with Lydcott they were tried in their absence, found guilty and hanged in effigy in the Royal Square, at the spot where the gilded statue of George II now stands. Chevalier reports that the wives of some of them remarked defiantly that though their husbands were hanging in the sun, the rain and the wind, they would not stop drinking the good red wine for all that!

Two avowed parliamentarians who did not flee the island were the Dean of Jersey, David Bandinel, and his son Jacques. David

Bandinel had been a poor Italian immigrant but subsequently gained great advancement through the patronage of, among others, William Laud, Archbishop of Canterbury, and Sir Philippe de Carteret. He quarrelled violently with the latter, for reasons unknown, and became Sir Philippe's worst enemy. Sir George imprisoned the Bandinels, first in Elizabeth Castle and then in Mont Orgueil.

Conditions were not, by the standards of the day, onerous. Their wives were allowed to visit them, to bring them food and clothing, and they were allowed to take the air on the battlements of the castle during the day. At night, it is true, they were locked in their room where they passed the time playing a game called 'tric trac'. They were also allowed visits by their friends – who must truly have been friends to be seen consorting with the known enemies of Sir George Carteret. From these men they discovered that the news from London was not good as far as they were concerned. The parliamentarians had condemned Laud to death. The archbishop had been instrumental in securing David's position as Dean of Jersey and the news of his imminent death put the fear of God into father and son. They feared, with reason, that terrible reprisals would be carried out on them and their families.

Escape became imperative. On the terrible night of 10 February 1645, with fear as the spur, they used a small gimlet to bore holes close together in the door of their cell and broke through with relative ease to a small room beyond. A latrine was built into the outer wall. They managed to prise loose some stones which gave them access to a high window many metres above the ground. They had found a large, metal soup ladle which they fixed as best they could into a crack or crevice in the wall above the latrine. This they used as a hook on which to fasten a makeshift rope of towels, clothes and cords. They hung the rope from the window down the castle wall. A fearful storm was blowing and the wind was howling round the castle fit to blow a man down. Trees were uprooted by its power and the seas were lashed into a frenzy. Chevalier describes the escape:

———————————————— ● ————————————————

But worse was in store, for at the foot of the wall, was a rough, steep and difficult rock which with a slope of earth fell precipitously down to the sea. And so they descended on this one, insecure rope. The son went first and found the rope too short. He crashed onto the rock and injured all his limbs. His father then tried to follow and climbing through the window endeavoured to lower himself down the wall, holding the rope in his hands with its end tied about him. When he was half way down however, the rope broke near the top and turning over and over, he fell headlong onto the rocks and there he lay with bones and body broken, unconscious.

———————————————— ● ————————————————

Jacques Bandinel crawled to his father, fearing he must be dead. David was alive, but he was unconscious, severely injured by the fall. The son turned his father on to his back and covered him with his cloak. Then he fled for his life.

The next day, the storm had abated. The dean was found by the castle guards just as Jacques had left him. For extra security while climbing out of the window, the old man had fastened the rope about his body but this had made the rope shorter and it was severely restricting his breathing. The guards loosened the rope and carried the dean into the castle. He was mortally injured. His wife was sent for, to come post-haste to her husband, and she arrived to watch over his dying. It took 24 hours. He did not speak or move, or indeed make any sign at all, and passed away on the morning of 12 February. He was buried in the parish of St Martin beneath a great thorn tree.

Jacques Bandinel was proclaimed a fugitive and an intense search followed. The harbours were closed, parishes were searched and a reward of 200 francs was offered for his capture. He was eventually discovered, suffering mightily from the effects of his fall, in a widow's house in the mid-island parish of St Lawrence. He was taken back to the castle to recover and convalesce, but a combination of the injuries sustained on that awful night and the fear of being tried by a royalist court finally killed him on the night of 18 March 1646.

Sir George Carteret was by now absolute monarch of Jersey in all but name. No one dared raise a voice of dissent if he levied new taxes to pay for continued resistance to Parliament. No one dared criticise him for fear of deportation. Nobody, least of all the States, dared object when he confiscated the lands and revenues of absent Jerseymen. And, of course, nobody made a fuss when his sea captains, armed with commissions from himself and the king, *lettres des markes*, brought back as prizes richly laden vessels and, occasionally, warships of the parliamentary persuasion. Chevalier's diary for the period is crammed with references to scores of such seizures. A ship captured in this way was brought to Jersey to be adjudged a lawful

The only portrait in existence of the great Sir George Carteret, in his manor house in St Ouen. He was a man of infinite resource and inestimable loyalty.

prize and once that process had been concluded the cargo was sold. Carteret naturally gained a share of the profits or, as in the case of a cargo of slate which he kept by for his own use in strengthening the fortifications of Elizabeth Castle, the cargo itself. Most of the wine in his cellar came from captured shipping.

For a time the seas around Jersey became very unsafe indeed. Nor were some of Sir George's captains averse to torturing crews into confessions of parliamentary allegiance – one test of what constituted a lawful prize. Several references are made in contemporary records to how burning fuses were put between men's fingers to force them into such admissions. However, very few of the hardy mariners confessed.

Things were indeed going very well for Carteret. True, there was always the worry of supplying Castle Cornet in Guernsey where the irascible Sir John Osborne was holding out for the king against the rest of Guernsey which had declared for Parliament. There was not much love lost between the two men, but Carteret knew very well that if Cornet fell the key to Jersey would be in parliamentary hands. With a safe harbour the parliamentarians could gather ships and men to launch an attack on a sister island. This was a far from pretty prospect and from self interest, not from any love, Carteret kept the Guernsey fortress as well supplied and secure as he was able.

However, things were not going well for the king's forces in England. Nor were they going well for Prince Charles. Parliamentary forces swept the boy's armies before them through Somerset, Devon and Cornwall until the future monarch found himself lord of no greater area than that of the Scilly Isles.

Small rock-girt islands, very pleasant for a holiday, the Scillies are hardly large enough, or indeed safe enough, to harbour a future king. The prince and his large retinue could expect no supplies from Cornwall. After the battle of Torrington in February 1646 the country was, with the noble exception of Pendennis Castle, entirely under the control of the all-conquering Thomas Fairfax, Commander-in-Chief of the New Model Army, and the parliamentarians. True, the prince's party had brought provisions of their own – wheat, milled flour, beef, butter and cheese – but these would not last long. The Scillies had a store of corn and an abundance of fish in the surrounding choppy waters, enough for the islanders' needs, but it is doubtful that they could have sustained the prince, his personal servants, divines, knights, squires, gentlemen and officials for any length of time, particularly if they were blockaded by the parliamentary navy sailing from Cornish harbours but a few miles distant.

The Governor of the Scillies, Sidney Godolphin, small of stature but loyal in spirit, had enough soldiers to man the tower and the island castle, but it was decided that even so the risks were too great for the prince and his retinue to stay. These fears were well founded. For the 6 weeks that the royalists stayed on the island, no supplies or provisions of any kind were allowed through to them. More ominous still, a large fleet of twenty-three ships had set sail to take the Scillies and capture the prince for Parliament.

Luck and bad weather favoured the young Charles. The parliamentary fleet was scattered by a great storm and on 15 April 1646 the prince, aboard the twenty-four-gun frigate the *Proud Black Eagle*, and accompanied by two smaller vessels, the *Doggerbank* and the *Phoenix*, managed to creep quietly and unseen from the islands. Two days later, on 17 April, they dropped anchor in St Aubin's Bay beneath the comfortable security of Elizabeth Castle. They had seen nothing more menacing on their crossing than three small boats sailing out of Guernsey.

There were very good reasons for sending the young prince, then about 16 years old, to Jersey. It would have been an admission of complete parliamentary supremacy to have him go into exile in a foreign country such as France or Denmark. For this reason, Charles I and his Council desired that the future king should be taken either to the Scillies or to Jersey. Exile in the Scillies was fraught with danger. Jersey was a much better option. It was well away from the Parliament-controlled mainland. It had two great castles, well provisioned and armed, which could be supplied from nearby France. Moreover, the lieutenant-governor and bailiff, Sir George Carteret, was a man of great skill and courage in matters of war and politics. He was also loyal beyond question. So it was the boy prince arrived in Jersey.

Resourceful and clever as he undoubtedly was, Carteret's skills must have been stretched to their very limits to organise an adequate welcome for so large a party – up to 300 strong – but he managed somehow. The prince and his immediate retinue were housed in the castle itself but, then as now, lodgings were in short supply and others in the royal party had to be content with rooms in the town. The prince had come with four great lords of the realm, appointed by Charles I to care for his son: Lord Hopton, a noble gentleman recently defeated by Fairfax at Torrington; Lord Capel and Lord Colepeper, the latter apparently with a temper more than equal to his name; and, last but by no manner of means least, the rotund, tiny, shiny-cheeked Sir Edward Hyde, one of the finest historians England has ever produced. He and Carteret became firm friends. Indeed Sir Edward embarked on his *History* at this time, and later built a fine house for himself in the grounds of Elizabeth Castle.

All was settled more or less. The prince was secure on Sir George Carteret's island, in Sir George Carteret's castle. Jersey life took a decidedly more royal turn. It is perhaps difficult for us, living in these egalitarian days of the twentieth century, to understand the divinity that did indeed hedge royalty in the seventeenth century, the awe in

Detail of the governor's residence in Elizabeth Castle, where the young Charles stayed in 1646. It shows a typical Jersey arch structure, executed in that pink granite that is so pleasing to the eye – and so expensive nowadays.

which kings and queens, princes and princesses were held and the real, tangible, political significance they possessed. Great court was paid to the princely visitor. Great ceremony attended almost his every move, most particularly when he dined. All the many dishes were presented on silver platters to the prince by kneeling servants, and the food he chose was tasted by another servant to make sure it wasn't poisoned. Likewise, his wine was first tasted by a young boy appointed specially for that purpose, who then held a silver bowl beneath the royal chin to prevent spillage down the royal clothes. A priest always stood close to Charles, on his right-hand side, and the company was completed by a small number of gentlemen-in-waiting, hovering with becoming deference to observe the royal eating habits.

There is more than a suspicion that the prince was bored with life on Jersey, and who could blame him if that were so? He was 16 years old and shut up in a forbidding fortress, surrounded by greybeards, forced to take part in protracted ceremonial and an unwilling player in the drama of England's destiny. Carteret solved the problem. He sent to St Malo and purchased a small pinnace for the young man, a very colourful design with the royal coat of arms across the stern. It had eighteen oars, two masts and velvet-covered seats for any guests the prince might take aboard. Charles took much delight in this new toy and particular pleasure in sailing it around and about St Aubin's Bay, himself at the helm. By this means he could relax from the more onerous royal duties such as attending the church at St Helier. Not but that his visits there are anything less than fascinating to us.

Chevalier, our trusty diarist, describes how the prince and his followers rode out along the causeway from the castle to that same church that still stands hard by the Royal Square. In those days, however, it stood by the shore with no buildings between it and the castle. With more and more land being reclaimed and more and more buildings and harbour works being constructed, the old church has receded further and further from the view of the sea and now cannot be seen from the castle. At the time of Charles' visit in 1646, however, he could ride direct, royal banners waving, 300 musketeers at hand, drums beating, from the castle, up the beach and directly into the church. His route was thronged with the people of Jersey who, though their loyalty to the king may have been a little suspect, thoroughly enjoyed a good spectacle. They crowded round the church as the prince entered to take his velvet-covered seat in front of the pulpit.

A bible, with all the passages to be referred to in the sermon carefully marked, lay on the table before him. A servant stood close by to turn the pages. Rose petals and sweetly scented herbs were scattered liberally about the prince. It was a sight indeed to be remembered.

Carteret meanwhile was busily raising the money to buy the food from Normandy to feed the great royal party – no mean feat. And, because he knew that the prince's presence on the island would inevitably provoke the unwelcome warlike attentions of the parliamentarians, he exercised himself mightily in strengthening the island's defences: St Aubin's Fort was strengthened with granite; the defensive and offensive capabilities of Elizabeth Castle were improved; a whole new fort – Fort Charles – was constructed at the north end of The Islet and another one was built at La Rocque. He ordered defences to be built at every vulnerable spot along the coastline. Jersey became a great fortress, as it was to be again during the Second World War, and was thought by some of the highest in the prince's Council to be impervious to any attack. Let the ships of the parliamentary navy flaunt themselves off St Ouen, even before Elizabeth Castle itself, flying the flag of rebellion – the prince himself was safe.

Indeed he was. But he was forced away from this island sanctuary to an even more oppressive sojourn with his mother, Queen Henrietta Maria, in Paris. For reasons already mentioned, this was thought to be a bad manoeuvre which would simply encourage the king's enemies to see their adversaries as being completely beaten, fleeing to sanctuary on foreign shores. Members of the prince's Council, including Hyde, tried to dissuade the king, and more especially the queen, from this course of action but it was all to no avail. The king wrote his queen a letter in which he said that their young prince should indeed go to Paris because, 'I think not Charles safe in Jersey'. There was an almighty row. Hyde believed that the king was misinformed as to conditions in Jersey and that if he had been rightly informed he would not so earnestly have wished his son to leave the island for France. The prince eventually decided to comply with what he saw as a direct command from his father, and preparations started to allow him to leave the kingdom completely.

His leaving took a little longer than expected. In fact, he was an unconscionable time going. On the morning of Tuesday, 23 June 1646, as his little fleet set sail to France, two parliamentary frigates of very warlike appearance sailed around Corbière Point and headed towards the castle to taunt the royalists as was their custom. The prince's boats, warned of imminent danger by the firing of the castle cannon and knowing they were no possible kind of match for the parliamentary ships, turned tail and scuttled in undignified fashion back to the port under the shelter of the garrison's guns. There they stayed all that day. Wednesday came, the weather was hideous and sailing impossible.

Thursday morning early, between three and four o'clock, the prince, now impatient with all delay, set sail. It was not to be. A powerful onshore wind sprang up from the south-east and beat him back to shore. They kept the ships anchored afloat, ready to sail at the first opportunity, and waited. For 17 hours they waited, until finally the royal prayers were answered. The wind suddenly blew storm force from the south-west. The opportunity to sail was there and it was not missed. The prince's fleet of nine boats, carrying all his baggage and followers, sailed before the wind for France and arrived 6 hours later, at eleven o'clock, in Coutainville. So ended Charles' first visit to Jersey.

Those lords who disagreed strongly with the decision to transport the prince into France remained behind. They included Edward Hyde in their number. Sir George continued about his business with undiminished vigour. He convened a meeting of the States to read a letter from the prince to the islanders thanking them for the protection and hospitality they had afforded him. Charles thoughtfully included the command that they should obey Lieutenant-Governor Sir George in all things. The good people of Jersey appeared to have little choice in this. They were compulsorily employed to perfect Carteret's plans.

Life settled back into something like routine. Carteret's wild sea captains continued to scour the seas for parliamentary ships. Those captured and adjudged to be lawful prizes of war continued to be sold along with their cargoes. Sir George's share of the booty, together with his share of the revenue of confiscated estates, undoubtedly laid the foundations of his considerable fortune. As Chevalier sagely remarks, 'Sir George made a fortune by stripping others.'

However, not all was perfect in Carteret's insular world. The natives were restless and, he suspected, not firm in their allegiance to the king, although he had done his best to ensure their loyalty. He had made them swear great oaths of fealty to the crown, not once but many times. He had hunted down and imprisoned those he suspected of parliamentary leanings. He had moreover, with great

Overleaf: Romantic view across St Aubin's Bay. Although it features a windmill in the foreground, there were far more watermills than *moulins* on Jersey when this picture was painted.

effort, produced the so-called Manifesto which was read to all the populace in every church on the island. In truth, it was little more than an extended exposition of Sir Philippe de Carteret's notion of a neutral Jersey. It is basically a declaration of absolute support for the king and his servants. The point is laboriously made that Jersey is a 'Peculiar' of the crown and historically part of Normandy, owing allegiance not to the English parliament but exclusively to the king.

Therefore it is the king, acting through his lieutenant-governor and his bailiff, who is the sovereign power; the English parliament has no right whatever to interfere in any way with the governing of the island. In other words, the quarrel between king and a parliament in which Jersey had no interest or representation was not Jersey's quarrel. Jersey was not party to it and, therefore, Jersey was a neutral in the story. In a just world the island should be allowed to get on with its life in peace.

Clever stuff indeed, but no one really believed it. Jersey was intrinsically bound up in the Civil War and the attempt to distance itself from the struggle was doomed to failure. Nevertheless, the assembled populace was required to sign the document in support of the monarchy. At first some refused saying they had no interest in fighting for either side, but in the end most signed. Sir George could be an implacable enemy. Chevalier remarks, rightly, that those of the royalist party who forced people to sign this manifesto made a miscalculation: although they 'secured the bodies of the people right enough, they did not secure their hearts, for each one [who] had signed and sworn fealty to His Majesty, there were numbers of others who had done the same through fear rather than conviction.'

That this was undoubtedly true became pitifully and painfully clear when Sir George Carteret was deserted by those on whom he should have most relied – his fellow Jerseymen.

The final, overwhelming attack from the parliamentary forces was, in the event, a long time coming but it didn't look that way at the end of 1646. A massive assault was expected daily. Pendennis Castle in Cornwall was finally taken on 17 August 1646. Everywhere Parliament was victorious, the royalists in disarray and ignominious exile. The king himself was a prisoner. Only a few, very small outposts – the Isle of Wight, Castle Cornet in Guernsey and, of course, Jersey – still offered any resistance. The time seemed ripe for a final mopping-up operation. However, it was not to be, and the reason was not far to seek.

The parliamentary party was deeply divided between those prepared to submit England to Presbyterianism in return for Scottish aid and the Independents who opposed them. These divisions prevented the vigorous pursuit of a coherent military strategy. True, the erstwhile commander of the island, Major Lydcott, not to mention the exiled and bitter committee members, constantly urged Parliament to mount an expedition to recover the island. And true, it was at last decided that a great force should be assembled in April 1647 to subdue Jersey. But the two Houses of Parliament could not agree on who should lead the force – Sir Hardress Waller, an Independent, or Colonel Aldridge, a Presbyterian. The divisions grew more pronounced. Pressing problems of dissension and strife between the army and Parliament had to be urgently resolved; recovery of Jersey slipped to the very bottom of every agenda.

Not being a man to spend too long on his knees thanking God for this respite, Sir George was soon up and about his and his master's business. That business had to do with Guernsey, lying flat and menacing along the horizon off the north-west coast. Only Castle Cornet was royalist; Sir George was going to take the rest of the island for the king.

He summoned the compliant States Parliament so that its members could rubber-stamp his plan to raise an expeditionary force of ships and men to attack Guernsey. This done, the soldiers, known as The New Soldiers of the Lieutenant-Governor's Company, who had been specially trained by Carteret's captains, were called to arms as were others from the twelve parishes. A fleet of eighteen ships – two frigates, a lightly armed galley and fifteen transports – was assembled. All was readiness. As Chevalier reports, 'The flower of Jersey manhood and the bravest of the land were prepared to go.' And go they did, sailing in warlike convoy on the evening-tide of Thursday, 20 August 1648.

It is often said, and with undeniable truth, that the greatest determining factor in the Channel Islands' history is the weather, which helps this or that party to unexpected victory. This occasion was no exception. The same stormy weather that had helped Prince Charles to escape from the Scillies now came to frustrate Carteret's grand strategy. The rain fell in sheets, drenching the soldiers and their powder. The sea got up and the wind roared from the west, blowing the fleet backwards, ever backwards, towards Jersey. Discouraged, sodden and simply unable to continue, Carteret turned his

Jersey has always been a fortress island. It is protected by the kind of stormy seas shown above and a largely impenetrable coastline with high, forbidding cliffs around the north coast as at Sorel Point (*right*) and dangerous rocks along the southern seaboard. Enemies might threaten but, with nature very much on the island's side, invasion was extremely difficult.

ships around and took them back home, vowing to try again another day. He courteously thanked his troops and gave them 5 sous each for their endeavours. He then enjoined them not to fail to answer the cannon's signal from Elizabeth Castle when it called them again to arms otherwise they would be shot.

On 27 August the cannon shot was heard, and the drums of muster throbbed in every parish. The troops filed down the valleys and the cotils, accompanied by the sound of tabor and violin, towards their embarkation points. As before, the fleet hoisted sail and set off for Guernsey. Again it was not to be. A great storm broke over the island, the rains again beat down mercilessly on the unprotected soldiery and the fickle wind blew up, this time from the south-west which was even worse than before. There was nothing for it but to return again to Jersey.

The days passed, four of them, but on the fourth day the wind blew from the south. This was ideal for sailing the fleet to Guernsey – or it would have been if it had not been gusting up to gale force and beyond. Passage was impossible for that day.

Only a little distracted from his purpose by the birth of a new daughter, Sir George waited for a favourable wind. It came, at last, on the morning of 29 August, but it was not until 30 August that the fleet managed to set sail for the third time. Sixteen vessels carried upwards of 1000 men-at-arms. Off Corbière Point, the rains came yet again to confound Sir George's purpose. The fleet was beaten back to port again. The storm was now so bad that many of the troops could not be disembarked until the next day to return to their homes and await the next summons.

Before that cannon signal could be fired Sir Baldwin Wake, who had replaced Sir John Osborne as Governor of Castle Cornet in Guernsey, came to Jersey on his way back from visiting the exiled Prince Charles. Sir George got on with Sir Baldwin as he had with his predecessor: very badly indeed. Sir Baldwin knew nothing of Sir George's plans to subdue Guernsey, but was incensed when he found out. He said that if anyone were going to reclaim Guernsey for the king it would be himself, and he did not need the help of George Carteret or, indeed, any Jerseyman; he did not trust the Jersey people and, if he wanted soldiers, he would go to the king for them, not to Sir George. Further, if Sir George dared come visiting Guernsey with soldiery he, Sir Baldwin, would fight him with all the powers at his command. Carteret was not going to be allowed the honour of subduing Guernsey. Sir George, as may be imagined, was not pleased; he was very angry indeed.

The wind blew fair for Guernsey on the morning of 12 September. A signal cannon was fired and yet again the drums beat in the twelve parishes calling the men to muster. But when they had done so, Sir George let it be known that, because of the jealousy of Sir Baldwin Wake and the irreconcilable differences between the two men, the expedition was called off, never to be remounted.

Thwarted by tempests on the one hand and Sir Baldwin's temper on the other, Carteret turned his attention to the smaller prize of Sark which also supported Parliament. There had been a previous attempt by royalists to capture this island in May 1645, but the invading force had been divided and finally defeated by troops from Guernsey. Sir George had a more than quixotic interest in Sark. Many revenues from the little island belonged to the Carteret family but had been lost when the Sarkese declared for Parliament. Money which would otherwise have gone to Sir George went instead to the Governor of Guernsey. However, like the invasion of Guernsey, this venture was doomed to failure, and for much the same reason: the weather. A small fleet of four frigates and four smaller transports carrying 300 men was duly assembled in Bouley Bay. But, as if by prearranged signal, the moment Sir George tried to put to sea on 19 September a storm blew up to prevent them going. When its intensity increased, and showed no sign of abating, the whole enterprise was called off and the men sent home. No further attempts were made to take Guernsey or Sark.

Sir George confined himself for the moment to Jersey business and, indeed, there was no part of island life that had not been in some way affected by him. Most of the time the island was on permanent alert for possible invasion, which meant great and very trying disruption of normal, everyday life. Young men from every parish had to present themselves for watch and ward duties all around the coast, every month of the year. Carpenters and masons were compelled to build and reinforce forts and castles. The money to pay for these warlike preparations came from specially imposed and greatly disliked taxes. It may be assumed that while the men and women of Jersey were compelled to maintain a public show of allegiance and loyalty to Sir George, their feelings in private were somewhat different.

However, even in private, great care was needed. Sir George had eyes and ears everywhere. If a person were discovered making traitorous remarks, an appearance in Sir George's new court house might result. The old Royal Court had been pulled down and a new court, as much a monument to Sir George as to justice, built in its place. Stone was brought in from the Mont Mado quarry and from nearer at hand in St Helier itself. The States Parliament ordered that every wagon should serve one day to transport the granite. In households where there was no cart or wagon, one man should be provided for one day's work. Anyone who did not wish to perform this onerous service could avoid it by paying 5 sous. Wood for beams and scaffolding was again taken in quantity from M. Herault's estate.

The most striking feature of the new building was a great, gilded iron crown on top of the belfry. In Chevalier's words: 'When the sun shone upon it it gave forth rays which dazzled the eyes of the spectators.' There it stayed, and there it shone, for all of Sir George's reign, a visible and potent reminder of his power and royal allegiance. The parliamentary army which came to conquer in 1651 tore it down and transported it to Guernsey. But that day was a long way off.

Overleaf: The great sandy bay of St Ouen, known as Five Mile Beach. At its centre is La Rocco tower, completed in 1801 and only recently restored.

Meanwhile, the unlucky and desperately isolated Charles I was in Carisbrooke Castle on the Isle of Wight as an unwelcome guest of Robert Hammond, the island's governor. Charles had by all accounts been trying desperately to get to Jersey and the welcome protection of Sir George, but Parliament had acted quickly to forestall him. The Isle of Wight was as far as he could get.

When Carteret received intelligence as to the king's whereabouts he mounted a rescue expedition. However, Cromwell was informed, in considerable detail, of Sir George's plan and it came to nothing. Perhaps Sir George would have been less anxious for the safety of his sovereign if he had known what Charles had agreed with Fairfax, as part of a proposed settlement: to have Sir George branded a criminal and banish him from England for the rest of his life, and to deprive the Carteret family of their estates for 3 years.

As it happened, none of Charles' machinations and secret deals with first one party and then the other came to anything. There were, it is true, small royalist uprisings but they were quickly and easily put down. More important, a renewed Scots invasion was completely and utterly defeated at the battle of Preston in August 1648. Cromwell now incarcerated the king in Hurst Castle, a formidable fortress on the Solent, but even so Sir George was seriously considering an all-out attack on the king's prison when events overtook him. The endgame had begun.

On 9 February 1649, two English gentlemen, Colonel Poulet and Mr Mohun, arrived on the island from Weymouth, via France. They had black scarves draped about their necks and wore black ribbons around their sleeves. They told how the king had been beheaded in Whitehall on 30 January. This was so monstrous that no one on the island knew whether their story could be believed. Sir George declared that he, for one, did not believe it and that no one else was to believe it either on pain of punishment. M. des Augres, old and infirm, was dragged into St Helier and imprisoned there for declaring his belief that the king was indeed dead. He was then banished from his own parish for the rest of his life. Three other 'simple fellows incapable of making trouble' (Chevalier) were exiled for life for declaring the same thing.

Rumour and speculation was, however, laid to rest on 16 February when Sir George received proof positive of the king's execution in the form of letters from Prince Charles' secretary in France.

The unfortunate Charles I. His inability to govern precipitated the Civil War and plunged Jersey into a decade of violence and disorder.

A NEW KING

On 17 February 1649 Sir George issued proclamations and fired cannon to announce the accession of King Charles II. Chevalier again: 'He lifted his hat and cried "Long live Charles II" and the people all shouted, "Long live King Charles" and threw their hats into the air.' Carteret had a new king to serve, and one who was to prove of inestimable value to him. However, the time for Sir George to claim the deserved reward for his heroic stewardship of His Majesty's Jersey had not yet come. The new king's situation was as difficult as his unfortunate father's had been before him, if not more so. The most promising support for Charles, in exile in Holland, seemed to come from Scotland where a force might be raised to restore a Stuart to the throne. However, the Scottish offer of support was so hedged about with impossible conditions that Charles, after due consideration, was forced to look elsewhere for succour. There was no way he could sign the Covenant and commit himself absolutely to Presbyterianism, as the Scots wished, without mortally offending all his would-be followers of different religious persuasions.

However, Charles had to move somewhere, even though his options were limited and fraught with danger. He could no longer stay in exile for his credit with his Dutch and French hosts had long since run out. Only Ireland, in all the British Isles, presented a possible opportunity for success. Royalist forces there were still intact and there were many of them. Furthermore, they were thought to be fighting quite successfully under James Butler, Earl of Ormonde, against the parliamentarians.

Jersey was considered to be a good step on the way to Ireland so the new king voyaged to the island with a retinue of up to 400 people, crammed into a fleet of twenty-one vessels. The 19-year-old king sailed himself to Jersey, standing at the helm of the royal, eighteen-oared galley that Sir George had thoughtfully provided for him during his last visit to the island. Charles II arrived in St Aubin's Bay on the afternoon of 17 September 1649, to the sound of many cannon fired from Elizabeth Castle and from the anchored ships. The Seigneur of St Ouen, inevitably a de Carteret, came to meet him. He rode into the sea until he was up to his horse's girth. He then bowed three times before the king as custom demanded.

Charles II came in even greater state than he had done before. Three magnificent coaches and their six attendant coach horses, jet black with white muzzles, were shipped from France. Many other horses were brought into Jersey: 129 fine, great war-horses in all, magnificent to look at but expensive to keep. It cost the parishes dear in contributions of hay and provender and there was much grumbling.

The king was, of course, still in mourning for his father's death and was dressed all in violet. To the left side of his cloak he wore a blue scarf and a silver star and round his left leg there was a blue garter. The royal retinue was dressed in black and the royal coaches were likewise draped in black. The sovereign and his retinue must have been an impressive and lavish spectacle, but their opulent appearance disguised the poverty-stricken reality. The royal coffers were absolutely empty. However, as ever, Sir George was at hand to give his lord and master financial support or, to be more precise, Sir George opened the purses of the Jersey folk and extracted the wherewithal to keep His Majesty in the manner to which he was accustomed. The tax on wheat was simply doubled to 20 sous a quarter. Even this did not, by any manner of means, produce enough money and the king remained in a very poor financial state for the duration of his stay in Jersey.

Charles' financial poverty was more than matched by the intellectual poverty of his close personal counsellors. The best of his advisers were absent. The astute Sir Edward Hyde was in Spain trying desperately to raise money for the penurious monarch, and Colepeper was in Russia on a similar mission. Those that remained included Lord Wilmot, Sir John Berkeley, Sir Edward Herbert and Lord Percy; a motley crew, characterised by drunkenness and a complete inability to grasp the political complexities and dangers of the king's position. Sir George could not have been pleased.

Events in Ireland took a disastrous turn for the worse. The all-powerful Cromwell had taken personal charge of the parliamentary forces there and had comprehensively and savagely routed the royalists, taking Tredagh with all manner of cruelty and butchery. Without stopping, he marched further into Munster. Disaffection among the royalist troops, and advance warning of the cruelty of Cromwell's forces, encouraged Cork, which might have offered stout resistance, to surrender without a shot being fired.

It was clearly out of the question for Charles to go to Ireland. He dismissed the two ships loaned by William, Prince of Orange, to take him there and he and his counsellors, such as they were, turned their attentions to other options – more fatefully again to Scotland.

It was a frustrating time. The king's beleaguered court was full of bickering, backbiting and bitchery. The royal party found Jersey rather dull. There was little of significance to do. Charles had to issue a stern decree against duelling; there were church services to be attended and, on 25 November, Sir George's new daughter was baptised at Elizabeth Castle. King Charles condescended to be god-father and further honoured Carteret by naming the child Caroline, the female form of Charles. This was a signal honour.

When Captain Antonio arrived in his frigate from Ireland, carrying 120 refugees driven out by Cromwell, this was further proof, if any were needed, of Cromwell's absolute ascendancy in that wretched country. It was at last decided to reach some accommodation with the Scots, although none of the difficulties attendant upon this had disappeared. A preliminary discussion with Scottish commissioners took place in December and a meeting was arranged between the king, the Scots and representatives of the English Presbyterians at Breda in Holland. Charles left for the meeting on 13 February 1650. He had spent almost 5 months in Jersey.

Before he left, the king gave Sir George the gift of Smith Island off the Virginia coast in the Americas. This was not such an extravagant gesture as might at first be supposed. It was a tiny place, just over 11 km (7 miles) long and under 1.5 km (1 mile) wide, and almost impossible to farm. None the less, undismayed, or perhaps ignorant of the nature of the island, Carteret despatched a boat full of people willing to settle on Le Nouveau Jersey as it had been re-named. They

Bonne Nuit Bay a century ago (*right*) and as it is today (*overleaf*), so called because Charles II is supposed to have bade the island farewell from here with those words. The story is almost certainly apocryphal, if touching.

were to be allowed free use of the land for the first 7 years but after that would pay Carteret a fixed rent in perpetuity. A good investment for Sir George. However, the best-laid plans of mice, men and Sir George often come to naught and this was an example. Just 12 hours after leaving the island the vessel was captured by a parliamentary frigate, commanded by Captain Green. The captain was in luck for the Jersey ship was a very rich prize. The passengers were stripped, their baggage was searched and they lost everything they possessed. Furthermore, the parliamentarians found, and confiscated, a large quantity of money belonging to Sir George. We may imagine that he was not best pleased.

With the king's departure, Jersey settled back into its old, insular ways and small concerns. However, the island's not inconsiderable fleet of privateers continued in the lucrative business of capturing parliamentary ships and taking their cargoes. Sir George could console himself with the thought that if Charles with his Scottish allies were victorious, he would instantly be rewarded for his services with the office of Treasurer of the Royal Navy and Vice-chamberlain of the Household. But it seemed highly improbable that Charles would succeed. The implication is that Sir George's devotion to the king was born not of ambition for advancement, although he would not be averse to this if it came his way, but rather of a principled devotion to the monarchy. The prospect of reward looked slim indeed and, sure enough, the grand alliance of the king and the Scots came to nothing when Charles' army was cut to pieces at the battle of Worcester on 3 September 1651. Cromwell, Lord Protector of England, now turned his attentions at last to the subjugation of George Carteret's Jersey.

THE PARLIAMENTARY INVASION

On 19 October 1651, the opening moves were made. A great fleet of eighty-six ships set sail from Weymouth under the command of the great Admiral Robert Blake. Sir George hurried to prepare for the onslaught. He sent his three youngest children to France. His wife and two other offspring remained in the castle. Lady Carteret refused to go, saying she would stay with her husband. Sir George brought large quantities of provisions over to Jersey from St Malo and strengthened all the fortifications of the island. He had two fire-ships constructed to attack the invading fleet. Further, he built ingenious mobile stockades, each large enough to conceal six musketeers while they fired on enemy troops.

On 30 October 1651, the impressive fleet sailed into St Ouen's Bay. Sir George was waiting for them. His cavalry, fusiliers and dragoons, and a force of Jersey militiamen raised from the twelve parishes were deployed along the sand dunes. That night, he ordered his fire-ships to attack the invading fleet, but his orders were not carried out by the Flemish crews.

Early on the following morning, the parliamentary commanders, Admiral Blake and Colonel Heane, sent representatives in a small boat to explore the possibility of a negotiated peace. Sir George was having none of this. He opened fire on the approaching vessel which hurriedly turned tail. The local Jersey militiamen, with little stomach for fighting a lost cause, were incensed at this and almost mutinied. A contemporary but anonymous chronicler records that the men called Sir George 'a man of blood' who would rather see them all killed than hear peace terms which would ultimately have to be accepted whether Sir George liked it or not. 'How can our tiny island resist three kingdoms?' they cried. 'We have reached the upmost limit of our loyalty, demand no more from us now.' In truth, the Jerseymen had had enough of the wars. They had also had enough of Sir George Carteret because of the heavy burden of taxation he had imposed upon them and the perpetual disruption to their normal lives. As Chevalier reports, 'The people were disgusted with him on account of the crafty manner in which he had taxed them and had long since tired of it all.'

So here were Sir George's men, hungry, cold and soaked to the skin in the steady October drizzle, led by a man they actively disliked and facing an overwhelmingly powerful battle-hardened enemy that had been everywhere victorious. They saw little if any hope of victory. They were right.

Some ships of the parliamentary fleet now moved around the headland towards St Brelade's Bay. Sir George, believing, probably rightly, that Heane and Blake were planning a landing, force-marched some of his troops there. However, no landing was attempted that day. Then a certain number of the fleet set sail for the eastern part of the island. Sir George did not know where the invasion would take place. He spent all that wet night of 31 October away from his men,

View across St Brelade's Bay, the most beautiful bay in Jersey, towards La Cotte, the great neolithic cave.

trying to see what was happening aboard the parliamentary ships. While he was so occupied, half his troops deserted.

At six o'clock on the morning of the next day, the remaining parliamentary ships sailed round to St Brelade's Bay and opened fire. Again, no attempt was made to land any troops. Perhaps the whole exercise was a feint to divide and dismay the Jerseymen. In any event, the fleet eventually withdrew from St Brelade and sailed back to St Ouen. Sir George was forced to march his men back there again. However, the fleet didn't stop in the middle of the bay as it had done before, but sailed towards L'Etacq in the north. Sir George dutifully marched his men along the coast in the same direction. But no sooner had the fleet reached the north end of the bay than it turned about and set a course towards the south. Sir George marched his troops back again. They did not go willingly.

This was their third day under arms. They had had little sleep, they were soaked to the skin, they were exhausted with marching up and down, they believed their cause was already lost and they disliked their leader. More than all these things, they were mortally afraid of the evident power of the enemy, sailing in ships the size and firepower of which they had never before seen.

All through that day the Jerseymen waited in the dunes. No attack came and night fell, inky black and cold. Suddenly, at 11 o'clock, the invaders arrived, yelling 'like Turks' (Chevalier) to put the fear of God into their opponents. Nevertheless, Sir George's cavalry charged among them and caused great destruction and confusion. Had there been other troops to press home this initial advantage there would have been a remarkable and famous victory. But most of the men who would have formed this second wave had deserted and the cavalry, with no support, was forced to retreat. Sir George fled immediately to Elizabeth Castle where preparations for the coming siege were well under way. Colonel Heane, meeting with no further resistance, occupied Jersey for Parliament. Sir George's reign was almost over. Almost, but not quite.

St Aubin's Fort, which had been so carefully strengthened, surrendered without a shot being fired. The twelve Jerseymen, one from each parish, who were supposed to defend it said they had never taken up arms against Parliament and were anyway unprovisioned to endure a long siege. The captain of the fort fled to Elizabeth Castle. Sir George wanted to hang him for deserting his post, and certainly the loss of St Aubin's Fort was a severe blow: it meant that the parliamentary fleet could have safe anchorage in St Aubin's harbour and safe passage all along the coast from Noirmont.

Mont Orgueil Castle was the next to capitulate. Sixty-seven Guernseymen imprisoned by Sir George and his captains were set free and joined with the rest of the invading marauders, pillaging the countryside. Nothing was safe, even beds and frying-pans were stolen. The Jersey women complained bitterly and directly to Colonel Heane about the wholesale looting. He did his best to restore the stolen property, but Chevalier mournfully records that there were such great numbers of troops involved and so many stolen items that it was impossible for anything like full restitution to be made. He also records that, 'There was a terrible waste of cider too, for an infinite quantity was drunk in three or four months, the year had been a great one for beer and cider and it was all consumed in a short time.' Jersey folk had good cause to curse the wars.

Sir George Carteret meantime was safe inside Elizabeth Castle, well supplied and with arms to withstand a long siege – or so he thought. Colonel Heane asked for his surrender. Sir George returned a dusty answer, saying he would never betray a king who had given him the task of defending the castle and that he would fight while his heart beat in his body. Battle commenced. Colonel Heane built powerful shore batteries by Westmount Town Hill (Mont de la Ville) and in St Helier churchyard. To build gun emplacements in the cemetery, it was necessary to excavate a great deal of earth and, in so doing, many graves were desecrated and the bones of the dead tossed about. The church itself was vandalised. The occupying soldiers used it as a latrine, broke up pews and the altar for firewood and stole the clappers and bell ropes from the two bells.

Sir George was, however, confident that he could successfully resist Colonel Heane's forces, and said as much in letters to the king who was now in France. His confidence would have been well founded were it not for three huge mortars that Colonel Heane had transported into Jersey. The biggest was capable of firing a 450 lb (200 kg) bomb containing 40 lb (18 kg) of gunpowder. Sir George was told of the existence of these awesome weapons, but chose to disbelieve the report. Proof positive was provided on 10 November when a huge bomb, aimed with deadly accuracy, fell through the roof of the old abbey church in the castle grounds, crashing through a lower floor and exploding in a powder magazine. Many men were killed by the huge blast and by tons of falling masonry. A great fire broke out and many of the castle's provisions were destroyed. Frightened for their lives, some of Sir George's soldiers attempted to flee. Five were captured, brought back to the castle and court-martialled. They were found guilty of desertion and sentenced to draw lots to see which two of them were to be hanged. One Englishman and one Jersey deserter were so condemned. The Englishman was rescued by his friends, but the wretched Jerseyman was hanged from the end of a cannon over the battlements.

If Sir George had intended to stiffen the sinews of his defending force, he failed miserably. The troops' morale plummeted, desertions continued and even Sir George must have realised that resistance was becoming increasingly impossible. He now sent his wife and two oldest children to France, where he had sent many of his prize possessions out of the grasp of the parliamentary army. He was operating a double standard: although he sent his own possessions to safety across the Channel, he would not allow other people in Jersey to send theirs.

Events were rushing to a climax. The mortars spread fear and destruction among the castle garrison as they rained down their huge bombs. Sir George, in desperation, sent to the king for help, but none was forthcoming. He was on his own. By the beginning of December, he recognised that all hope of lengthy resistance had disappeared.

Sir George decided to send a boat, loaded with five casks of whale oil to pay for the hire of some troops, to France. He also put on board a quantity of his own silver plate and two expensive chargers, as well as other personal property. We may believe that the cargo was worth a great deal to him. The vessel did not get far. The wind blew up from the south and forced her aground on the island bridge or causeway which joins Elizabeth Castle to the mainland. When the tide retreated, she was stranded. The parliamentarians immediately opened fire on her but had little success. If nothing was done, the boat would escape on the next tide.

Colonel Heane offered the not inconsiderable reward of £3 to any man who could set her alight under cover of darkness. He got his volunteer. On the night of 5 December the plucky chap crept unseen up to the beached vessel with 'bottles of inflammable material' (Chevalier) and succeeded in setting it alight. The conflagration was spectacular. The flames from the burning wood and whale oil melted the silver plate, burnt Sir George's other possessions and destroyed his horses. There was little left when the tide returned.

Charles II. As Prince of Wales he was bored in Jersey – but grateful for the protection the island and, more particularly, Sir George Carteret afforded him.

Sir George, with a dwindling stock of food, an increasingly mutinous garrison, unable to reply to the mortar bombardment and with no hope of help was forced to surrender. It has to be said that the terms were exceptionally favourable. The officers and soldiers were to march out of the castle with the full honours of war, drums beating and colours flying. The officers would be permitted to retain their swords, pistols and breast-plates and the soldiers could keep their swords. Everyone would be allowed to retain clothing, papers and counter books. Anyone wishing to go to France or England would be provided with passports, free transport and food for the journey. Favourable terms indeed, but Sir George obtained the best for himself.

Chevalier recalls hearing that Colonel Heane gave Sir George £1800 as an inducement to surrender the castle, although no record of this transaction is in the published 'Terms for the Surrender of Elizabeth Castle'. These terms left Sir George to walk absolutely free with his wealth, estates and possessions intact, and allowed him to sail on Monday 15 December to St Malo in his own ship 'with the reservation of Sir George's baggage and silver plate belonging to him personally'.

On the appointed day, great crowds gathered to watch him depart. They pressed forward on the sands. Colonel Heane considered they were getting too close to the castle and fired a single cannon ball at them. The projectile bounced off a horse and into the sea. The wretched creature was killed.

In the event, it was not until the following day that the wind stood fair for France and Sir George sailed away from the little island he had held so long, and so faithfully, for a defeated king. His reward was to come.

SIR GEORGE AT COURT

Like his famous countrywoman Lillie Langtry two centuries later, Sir George never did anything for nothing. True, he was a courageous and resourceful royalist through and through. But he made sure that every penny he spent in the king's cause was recorded and, when the time was due, he demanded and received complete repayment. He did his considerable best to save the king. The king in return made him a fortune.

After the taciturn, phlegmatic General George Monck had restored Charles II to the throne in 1660, Carteret ran to his sovereign with all the alacrity of Falstaff to Henry V, but with much better hope of advancement. The coronation, fittingly enough, was on St George's Day, 23 April 1661, and Sir George cut an impressive figure in the procession.

It was a time of national rejoicing. As Charles had promised, George was appointed Vice-chamberlain of the King's Household. This was a highly lucrative post. Lord Clarendon who, as Sir Edward Hyde, had been an honoured guest and friend of Carteret at Elizabeth Castle during the king's boyhood exile, managed to get him a place on the Privy Council. This was an exceedingly important elevation for Sir George; the Council was the very heart of government. Even more, he became an important member of that council within the

Charles II's magnificent coronation procession in 1661, in which Carteret figured prominently. Sir George reaped a rich reward for his outstanding loyalty to the king.

Council known as the Cabinet. There was no matter of policy in which he did not have a voice, and a powerful one at that. He had achieved his ambition: 'That the King shall not be able to whip a cat but I mean to be at the tail of it.'

Sir George did not care to return to Jersey. He relinquished the office of bailiff, to another de Carteret needless to say, and devoted himself entirely to his new and prosperous life in England. He was a busy man. As well as being vice-chamberlain to the king, he became Treasurer of the Royal Navy, a post to which, given his background, he was eminently suited. He did the job well by all accounts and the job did well by him. He was provided with a fine house at Deptford and was permitted three pence of every pound that passed through his department. At a conservative estimate that gave him an income, huge for the time, of £8000 a year. This, together with the income from his other appointments and from the recovery of sums lent out in the years before the Restoration, made Sir George Carteret a very rich man indeed. He was flying high, but he made enemies – and powerful enemies, too. He even quarrelled with his old friend Lord Clarendon, who had eased his progress to the Privy Council. More seriously, he ruffled the feathers of the all-powerful Lord High Admiral, the Duke of York – Charles' brother and the future James II.

The outbreak of the second of the Dutch Wars in 1664 ushered in the darker period in his fortunes. The Exchequer had little money to finance a naval war and no one, it seemed, was prepared to lend a sou to Charles.

The government was virtually bankrupt. Charles II, like his father before him, was compelled to recall Parliament to vote for fresh supplies, particularly for the navy. It was remarked that while the Royal Navy had no money at all, the treasurer of the navy was by contrast a fabulously wealthy man. Was there some connection between the two facts? Was Sir George redirecting funds intended for the navy into his own pocket? It was a good question. Even the loyal Pepys remarks on Carteret's secretive accounting methods. Sir George was called to give an account of his activities before a specially appointed Parliamentary Committee. At this critical juncture, however, the king, having obtained supplies and ever Carteret's friend, instantly prorogued Parliament. The committee was consequently disbanded. However, the suspicions and accusations did not go away. Far from it.

Meanwhile, the war with Holland had taken a turn for the worse. On 12 June 1667, the Dutch, under their intrepid commander de Ruyter, sailed up the Medway without let or hindrance. Not so much as a musket was fired. They sank more than a dozen ships and took prisoner the pride of the English fleet, the *Royal Charles*, towed her down the river and burnt her. The humiliation was complete.

Sir George resigned his office, but he could not escape another committee of inquiry. He was found guilty on several charges though it is extremely doubtful that he had indeed embezzled, or mishandled in any way, any of the money that passed through his hands. Nevertheless, ruin and ignominy stared him in the face. The House of Commons fully intended to impeach him and strip him of all his offices. Again the king, proving as much Carteret's friend as Carteret had been his, prorogued Parliament before anything more could be done. Charles went further, declaring that he himself vouched for the integrity of his old friend so any further inquiry into the handling of navy funds was superfluous and, moreover, an insult to His Majesty. Sir George had escaped – but only just. It was the end of his career. He had escaped impeachment but never again held high office. Although he continued to sit in Parliament, he was no longer a member of the Privy Council and his place on the Admiralty Commission was filled by someone else.

Sir George was put out to grass. He died peacefully in January 1680, and is buried in the Carteret chapel in Haynes (formerly Hawnes) Church, Bedfordshire. He had performed great services for the king when all others had deserted him. Charles repaid those services tenfold, according to his promise: 'If God bless me you shall find I do remember them to the advantage of you and yours and for this you have the word of your ever loving friend Charles R.'

3

THE GREAT PRETENDER
Philippe d'Auvergne
(1754–1815)

The Russian empress, Catherine II (the Great), received the officers from the frigate HMS *Flora* in her palace in St Petersburg. They saw a very handsome and very powerful woman. She had deposed her violent and drunken husband, Peter III, and had ruled Russia since 1762. As well as being an astute politician, Catherine was a deeply sensual woman who enjoyed many men and youths, loving them and casting them aside with equal facility.

One of the very junior officers presented by the British Ambassador, Lord Cathcart, to Her Majesty on that day in 1772 was a young midshipman, Philippe d'Auvergne, from Jersey, an island of which the empress had never before heard. She was very impressed by him. He was 18 years old, tall with brown hair and piercing blue eyes but, more than that, he had an extraordinary winning charm for one so young. The empress was captivated. She wanted him as a lover and a courtier, and to that end he was discreetly asked if he would consider entering her service. The youth respectfully declined, and returned with his fellow officers to the *Flora* anchored off Kronstadt. They then set sail across the Baltic Sea for Copenhagen. Philippe's great charm was to impress all the people he met.

Philippe d'Auvergne was born in Elizabeth Castle on 22 November 1754, on the island of Jersey. His father was Charles d'Auvergne and his mother, Elizabeth, was the daughter of Jersey's lieutenant-bailiff, Philip le Geyt. Charles had a distinguished military career serving with distinction under Lord Howe, First Lord of the Admiralty and 'Black Dick' to his men. Howe was one of the most respected and loved mariners of his time. He was not given to making long speeches, but his actions bespoke a grave, clever and loyal man. He rewarded

Charles' devotion by procuring the advancement of his sons and daughters.

In particular, he helped Philippe. Charles d'Auvergne had to resign his commission because of ill health, and was given a delightful sinecure in the ordnance department of Jersey. Tragically, Elizabeth died soon after Philippe came into the world but, 3 years later, his father married another Elizabeth – Elizabeth Bandinel, daughter of Seigneur de Melesches.

The d'Auvergnes lived frugally enough, for they were by no means rich, in a small house on the east of the island facing the French coast which, on a good day, could be clearly seen. In 1756, when Philippe was 2 years old, the Seven Years War with France began. Again, as in the past, the islanders mounted anxious and constant watch in the well-founded belief that an invasion might come at any time.

A NAVAL CAREER

Like Sir George Carteret before him, Philippe's natural inclination was not to be a soldier but rather to be a sailor in the king's navy, an ambition that was fulfilled with the help of the family friend Lord Howe. He secured the 15-year-old boy a lowly position on board the royal yacht, the *Mary*.

This was a gentle prelude to what was to become a very warlike career; the royal yacht was manned by a picked crew and the worst horrors of naval life, such as flogging round the fleet and keelhauling, were not much in evidence. True, the captain was an uncouth fellow, but he was not devoid of a sense of humour. It is told that some years before he had distinguished himself mightily in a battle against the French. His friend Lord Anson, who had also been involved in the action, remarked to him that the king would knight him for his heroic service. 'Troth me Lord, I ken nay use that'll be tae me,' replied Captain John. 'But no doubt your wife would be pleased at being my lady,' reasoned Lord Anson. 'Weel then,' the captain rejoined, 'His Majesty may knight her if he pleases.'

Young Philippe next joined the frigate HMS *Flora* as a midshipman: again, he owed his appointment to the good offices of the bluff Lord Howe. It was in this vessel that he voyaged to Kronstadt and saw, and so impressed, the Empress Catherine. In Copenhagen,

Elizabeth Castle as it was in 1764 when Philippe d'Auvergne was 10 years old. In those days he little dreamed of the adventures that lay ahead.

on the return voyage from the freezing northern waters, the *Flora* docked in the next berth to *Le Flou,* a French frigate. This would have mattered little, but on board *Le Flou* was a team of French scientists from the Académie des Sciences in Paris. Philippe became passionately interested in the problems of accurate navigation which they were addressing. He was more than a little helped by his ability to speak fluent French – it was, after all, his native tongue. The young midshipman became so absorbed with these questions that, once back in London, he sought out teachers to help and instruct him instead of heading for the nearest bar or bordello. As the *Naval Chronicle* reports, he 'prosecuted his studies in mathematics under the most celebrated professors in London.' With a great deal of success it would seem.

As a direct result of his academic endeavours, and with a little help from Lord Howe, he was appointed midshipman aboard the *Racehorse,* under the command of Captain John Phipps, later Lord Mulgrave. Phipps was to lead the *Racehorse* and her sister ship, the *Carcass,* on an expedition to see how close it was possible to sail to the North Pole. Even more exciting they were to try and discover if there was such a thing as a Northeast Passage to India and China. On the voyage as many experiments were to be carried out, and observations made, as possible.

It must have been a hugely exciting propject for the young Philippe as the two ships hoisted sail on 2 June 1773 and set a course due north into the unknown. If he looked over his shoulder, Philippe could have seen, a little to the rear, the *Carcass,* on which the 15-year-old Horatio Nelson was serving.

The further north they voyaged, the more difficult conditions became. The ice began to thicken and fog shrouded the two boats so thickly they could not see each other, indeed, on one occasion, they crashed into each other. Luckily, no serious damage was done and they continued on the voyage. On 24 July, disaster struck. A strong current swept the two vessels into a small bay and, before they could turn about and escape, ice-floes crashed together behind them, riding one on top of another to form a great barrier dozens of feet high. They were trapped. They had no dogs or sledges and the terrible Arctic winter was coming in. The prospect was bleak and the danger so apparent that Captain Phipps took the courageous decision to abandon ship. The crews lowered the longboats on to the ice. The idea was to manhandle these across the ice barrier to open water, in

A graphic illustration of the conditions encountered by the *Racehorse* and *Carcass* as they sailed through the far and frozen north seas. Members of the expedition included d'Auvergne and Horatio Nelson.

the rather forlorn hope of being picked up by a whaler that might still be cruising in these far northern latitudes. The odds on discovering such a ship were long indeed.

Pushing and shoving the boats laden with provisions across the far-from-smooth packed ice proved almost impossible. They inched forward. After almost 8 hours they had managed to progress only a few hundred yards.

Night was falling and the men were resting on the ice, frozen and exhausted, when suddenly the great barriers of ice began to crack and separate. The *Carcass* and the *Racehorse* were miraculously floating free. Crew, officers and captain stumbled and scrambled back to the ships as fast as they were able, clambered aboard with all expedition and hoisted sail. They ran before the wind as fast as they could, away from the harsh northern latitudes southward to aptly named Fairhaven in Norway, where they dropped anchor on the morning of 12 August. Enough was enough. Phipps abandoned the attempt to find the fabulous Northeast Passage and ran for home.

For Philippe d'Auvergne, however, the expedition had been very much a success. He had distinguished himself in all manner of ways. Captain Phipps liked him and his work enormously, and used Philippe's original sketches for engravings illustrating the graphic account of the voyage published in 1774. George III himself had commanded this publication, and was much impressed by it. His Majesty was to remember the name d'Auvergne in later years.

Philippe remained on shore for almost a year after his adventure to the deep north, pursuing his mathematical studies with vigour. However, his sojourn in London was rudely interrupted by events half a world away across the Atlantic.

The American colonies were in revolt, and with good reason. The British Government tried to impose taxes on the 13 colonies. They demanded a voice in the British Parliament if they were to be taxed. The colonies' position was clear: no taxation without representation. Their determination was underlined when the Bostonians threw a cargo of tea into the harbour, refusing to pay the threepenny duty which had been imposed. The War of American Independence had begun.

A small fleet under Admiral Thomas Graves was hurriedly despatched across the Atlantic to bring the colonists to heel. Philippe d'Auvergne sailed with that fleet aboard the *Aisha,* under the command of Captain van de Put. He was to spend 4 years in America, in the thick of the action.

In April 1775 a force of 800 British troops, under the command of Lieutenant-Colonel Smith, advanced on the little town of Concord, 20 miles from Boston. General Thomas Gage, commander-in-chief in North America, had received intelligence that a large store of arms and powder was hidden there. The troops were ferried part of the way and d'Auvergne commanded one of the boats. Not content to wait behind while the soldiers advanced, he and several of his fellow naval officers went along with the force to observe the spectacle. Under cover of night, the British troops attacked. They were expected. Paul Revere, by his famous ride, had forewarned the townsfolk and they were prepared for the onslaught. There was a savage and bloody battle at Lexington with the colonial militia. The British at last managed to get through to Concord, and destroyed the munitions. But on the way back they were harried and harassed at every turn. There was no rock, bush or tree that did not conceal a sniper. The British troops were unable to respond to these guerrilla tactics. Their losses mounted and the retreat turned into a rout, with over eighty men killed and nearly 200 injured. Philippe d'Auvergne and his fellow officers escaped only by the skin of their teeth. The battle for America was joined in earnest – and very unpleasant it was.

Philippe d'Auvergne was involved in two savage acts of reprisal.

In October 1775 a British officer was captured and imprisoned for a while in the town of Falmouth in Maine. Gage's successor as commander-in-chief, General William Howe, with a stupidity born of arrogance, ordered the town razed to the ground. A squadron of four ships, including d'Auvergne's ship, the *Preston,* was sent on this nefarious errand. The town, now called Portland, was mercilessly bombarded for 3 hours, after which soldiers landed and set fire to the wooden houses. Little remained but death, ashes and bitterness.

Even worse was the fate that befell the town of Norfolk in Virginia, in December of that same year. The townspeople had refused to supply the British forces with provisions. Swift punishment followed. Three warships, the *Kingfisher,* the *Otter* and the *Liverpool,* first bombarded the town and then sent raiding parties ashore to burn all that was left standing. The fighting was fierce, much of it hand to hand, as the townspeople struggled fiercely and heroically to save their homes. It was not to be. The town was burnt so completely that not a house or building of any kind remained. When d'Auvergne and the Royal Naval Squadron set sail away from Norfolk, they left nothing but smoking ruins. The action had precisely the opposite effect of that intended by General Howe. Instead of forcing the colonists into submission and compliance, it stiffened their resolve, making them doubly determined to beat the British out of the New World.

Philippe was now 20 years old. He had served in the Royal Navy with great distinction for 5 years. By way of reward, he was given command of his own ship: the *Alarm.* It was a small vessel which had been armed and modified for river patrol. He had no sooner got his ship, however, than he lost her.

The French and Spanish, ever anxious to fish in troubled waters, entered the war on the colonists' side at the beginning of 1778. On 28 July Admiral Charles D'Estaing and a powerful French fleet arrived off New York. Two large frigates sailed up the river and effectively trapped the *Alarm* and two other ships: the *Kingfisher* and the *Spitfire.* The surprise was complete; there was no escape. D'Auvergne reluctantly gave the order to run the *Alarm* aground on Rhode Island. He offloaded his cannon and landed his crew, then deliberately set the ship – his first command – alight. He sat and watched her burn.

Philippe did not stay much longer in America after this catastrophe. He served for some time in the Rhode Island shore battery, and then, like all captains who have lost their ships, he was court-martialled. He was acquitted of any blame by the court, which found he had acted properly in preventing the *Alarm* from falling into enemy hands. Immediately after the hearing, Philippe headed back to London in the warship *Leviathan*. His fame had gone before him.

D'Auvergne had had a good war. He was wounded only once, and that but slightly at Falmouth. More important, he distinguished himself in every operation in which he was involved. It was not just his skill as a fighting man, however, that gained him recognition and advancement. His diplomatic abilities were also put to good use. The *Naval Chronicle* records that Admiral Sir Peter Parker employed him to 'execute several commissions from the Admiral and the General to the American Government at Providence. These he performed much to their satisfaction.'

A grateful Admiralty soon gave him the post of first lieutenant on board the thirty-two-gun frigate the *Arethusa*. It was no easy assignment. The *Arethusa* was part of the Channel Fleet, which was locked in a ferocious and seemingly losing battle with a decidedly superior French naval force. It was a dangerous time to be at sea.

In February 1779, the *Arethusa* was involved in a hard-fought action with the French frigate *L'Aigrette*. The battle lasted for 2 hours with neither ship gaining the upper hand. The *Arethusa*, however, was badly damaged and, when a storm blew up, she was driven ashore and wrecked off Ushant. The survivors were captured by the French and imprisoned in Carhaix in Brittany. The aftermath of these events changed Philippe's life forever, making him first a prince and finally a pauper.

THE DUKES OF BOUILLON

Before the map of Europe was redrawn at the Congress of Vienna (1814–15), there were a number of small, independent principalities in existence. The Ancient Duchy of Bouillon, to the east of Luxembourg and the south-west of Flanders, was one such little state. It was very small – about three times the size of Philippe's native Jersey – with a population of about 11 000, mostly employed as farmers. The countryside was extremely attractive, consisting of extensive woodland on the high ground and small picturesque farms in the long valleys. Its capital, Bouillon, was built in the valley of the river

The *Arethusa*. Philippe joined her when her reputation as scourge of the French fleet had already been achieved.

Semois and was overlooked by a forbidding fortress which had once served as home to the old dukes of Bouillon whose lineage stretched far back to the great crusader Godfrey de Bouillon. The duchy was famous as a refuge for dissidents and radicals of all kinds. Towards the end of the eighteenth century its printing presses were churning out atheistic, radical, revolutionary and dissident publications of all kinds, plus a little pornography on the side – very rare in those repressed times. Jean-Jacques Rousseau wrote his *Confessions* there, and the brilliant Voltaire holidayed at length in this oasis of freedom.

In 1678, Louis XIV of France had given the duchy as a reward to his Grand Chamberlain, La Tour d'Auvergne. He and successive d'Auvergnes ruled for the next 100 years, but from afar. Their main possessions and interests were in Normandy and they did not often visit their northern duchy, preferring to stay in the sumptuous splendour of the Château de Navarre, built in the country between Rouen and Paris and overlooking the Iton valley.

It was a great château, with Italian marble floors and huge mirrors. Its focal point was a spacious central area under a richly decorated dome called the 'Hall of Guards'. It was hung with flags, portraits and all the heraldry of the d'Auvergnes, stretching back through the ages. Dozens of rooms, each fabulously decorated and furnished with rich materials from the four corners of the world, adjoined this great hall. Outside, the grounds were extensive, to put it mildly. The little village of St Germain de Navarre had been absorbed completely into the estate, and surrounded with an exotic garden, *Le Jardin d'Hebe*. This contained great pools teeming with goldfish, orangeries and orchards, hothouses and fountains. Everywhere were statues of mermen and mermaids, artfully positioned around and beneath artificial waterfalls. It was an extraordinary château and its fame, bruited far and wide, excited the curiosity of many a traveller.

In the late eighteenth century, the ruler of Bouillon was Charles Godfrey de La Tour d'Auvergne, a splendid old fellow. However, at the time of Philippe d'Auvergne's incarceration in Carhaix he was a far from happy man, despite his great wealth and possessions. His first wife had left him because of his persistent infidelities. Of the two sons he had by her, the older boy was killed in childhood while the younger son was hideously disfigured. Jacques-Leopold had a huge hump on his back, he could not speak properly, he slobbered, he had no legs at all and had to be wheeled everywhere in a huge chair. Jacques was also impotent. The duke despaired for the continuation of the d'Auvergne dynasty; on Jacques' death there would be no one to carry on the line.

The duke could see but one solution, and that was to adopt an heir. Certainly, this had been custom and practice in Roman times, but whether it could legally be done in eighteenth-century France was open to question. Needs must, however, and the duke embarked on the search to find a successor. He wanted someone from a branch of his own family and, to this end, he employed his old teacher, the Abbé Coyer, to conduct the search. The abbé was a meticulous academic, and archivist of note, who had made a special study of the d'Auvergne family and ancestry. He assembled a team of researchers and they began their search for a suitable d'Auvergne to inherit Bouillon and Navarre. They searched in every library. They enquired

The great crusader, Godfrey de Bouillon, who may have been Philippe's ancestor.

in every town and every church without success. The process dragged
on and on. The duke's great quest to find an heir became known
throughout the land. The French Government knew of it, and sym-
pathised with his predicament. In particular, M. de Sartine, the French
Naval Minister, was aware of the good old duke's search.

M. de Sartine read – we may believe with a great deal of satisfaction – the list of British officers and crew who had been taken
after the notorious *Arethusa* had been wrecked, and who were now
imprisoned in Carhaix. He saw the name d'Auvergne on the list and
at once wrote to the duke in Navarre, informing him of this strange
coincidence. The duke was tremendously excited, and contrived to
get Philippe released on parole and brought to Navarre.

That first visit to the magnificent château must have astonished
Philippe, so lately penned-up in a tiny cell with little or no hope of
early release. The assiduous abbé was ordered to begin investigations
into the Jersey d'Auvergnes to see if they were related in any way to
the d'Auvergnes of Navarre. The duke must have hoped against hope
that the abbé's research would bear fruit, for Philippe impressed him
with his charm and wit and with an intellect unusual in such a young
man. He was the very opposite of his own unfortunate son. Philippe's
hopes must have echoed the older man's. The duke's lands, palaces
and estates would be a prize rich beyond the dreams of avarice.

The duke performed a signal service for Philippe at this time. He
applied to the French Government that he be exchanged for a French
prisoner. The request was granted and Philippe, his head full of novel
thoughts, departed Navarre for England, while the abbé and his
myriad helpers embarked on the task of establishing his claim to the
duchy of Bouillon. It was to be a long process.

Philippe d'Auvergne took up his naval career again with relish.
He saw action off the Cape of Good Hope, and distinguished himself
by capturing four Dutch ships of the line. In 1782 he was in the South
Atlantic, in command of HMS *Rattlesnake*. The ship was part of a
small fleet commanded by Commodore George Johnstone, an officer
of dubious ability and uncertain judgement. He had been completely
out-manoeuvred and defeated by the French off the Cape and, for this
reason, his professional future looked a little bleak. On 6 June 1782,
the squadron fetched up by Trinidad – not the West Indian Trinidad,
but a tiny, uninhabited, volcanic island. It was a truly inhospitable
place, with vicious rocks full of dead trees and thousands of huge,
predatory, yellow crabs that attacked everything that was in their

way, including the mariners. Johnstone, however, saw it as a means to restore his fortunes in the eyes of the Admiralty. He would claim this miserable rock for Britain, even though he was told of its unsuitability for colonisation. As the *Naval Chronicle* records, 'He affected to view it as a jewel fit to adorn the British crown. He gave orders to Captain d'Auvergne to stay and maintain possession of it until His Majesty's ministers should determine from his report whether he should retain possession.' Having ordered Philippe to stay behind with Captain Pasley who commanded the *Jupiter*, Johnstone disappeared towards England.

The next 14 months were the most uncomfortable of d'Auvergne's life. The privations and hardships he had to endure permanently undermined his health and made him that much less able to face the struggles ahead.

Disaster struck almost immediately after Johnstone's departure. On the night of 12 October, d'Auvergne was on shore, guarding supplies, when a great tropical storm blew up. Mountainous seas pounded the *Rattlesnake* and snapped her cables. The anchor would not hold. The master, who had remained on board, tried in vain to head the ship out to sea, away from the dangerous, rocky shoreline, but, seeing this was a hopeless endeavour, took the only course open to him. He tried to run the ship ashore on a small sandy beach. It was a prodigious feat of seamanship. He managed to squeeze the vessel between the rocks and land the crew safely. The *Rattlesnake*, however, was smashed to pieces on the beach. The cannon were saved, and many of the timbers from the wreck were used later to make shelters.

D'Auvergne was left with his crew of thirty men, but without a ship. Captain Pasley, who had been ordered to leave Trinidad, offered d'Auvergne the chance to leave with him. Philippe, obeying to the letter his instructions from Johnstone, declined the offer and stayed.

It seems that he and his men were forgotten. Captain Pasley and his crew paid a brief visit 2 months later, in December, and landed a few supplies but they were not enough. The food was soon consumed and attempts at farming failed utterly. The beleaguered sailors were reduced to living off wildfowl, fish and the bitter-tasting crabs that swarmed everywhere. Months passed. It seemed as if help would never come. When it did, it was by pure accident. The fifty-gun battleship, *Bristol*, and a convoy of Indiamen outward bound from England to India, were blown far off course and hove to off Trinidad on 20 September 1782. The would-be colonists were rescued from further suffering and taken on to India.

Again, Philippe faced a court martial for the loss of a ship. He was again acquitted of any dereliction of duty. Indeed, he received glowing praise, as the *Naval Chronicle* reports: 'His passive and respectful deference to the most extraordinary commands ever given by a superior officer to a professional inferior gained high commendation and were ever after remembered by his gracious Sovereign who granted him post rank when he returned from India in January 1784.' It was a triumphant return. The path to great advancement was now open to him. Even better news greeted him when he reached London.

The old Duc de Bouillon was waiting for him with the glad tidings that the Abbé Coyer's efforts had been crowned with success. He claimed to have proved conclusively that Philippe d'Auvergne was indeed related to the d'Auvergnes of Navarre, and closely enough related for the duke to adopt him as a son. The duke presented Philippe with a bust of the d'Auvergnes' greatest ancestor, Turenne, in celebration of the event. It bore this inscription, stating that the duke's gift was a token of his affection for his adopted son:

TURENNE
Donné à Philippe d'Auvergnes CDVASDLGB
Par Godfrey Duc de Bouillon
Chef de la Maison en témoignage de sa tendre amitié
pour son fils adoptive
mdcclxxxiv

The initials after Philippe's name stand for *Commandeur de vaisseaux au service de la Grande Bretagne*.

The world was at his feet, but he was in poor health after his miserable experiences in Trinidad. The duke invited him to Navarre to rest and recuperate and contemplate his inheritance, and he duly went there in the winter of 1785. The old duke appraised George III of his hopes that Philippe would succeed him in the duchy of Bouillon. The king, mindful of the young man's outstanding service to the crown, gave his formal support and recognition to Philippe's new and elevated position. In 1786, the duke signed documents formally adopting Philippe as his son, now entitled to use the d'Auvergne family motto: *Nous ne changeons pas* (We do not change). In 1788,

Henri de La Tour d'Auvergne, Vicomte de Turenne. The family's greatest ancestor, he was appointed Marshal of France in 1643.

he drew up his last will and testament, leaving to Philippe the sword of the great Turenne. The Jerseyman could look to the future with confidence.

Unfortunately, events began to conspire against the fulfilment of his dreams. In 1790, the ill health that had dogged him since 1782 forced him to relinquish the command of the frigate *Narcissus*. At that moment, he received a summons from the old duke to come to Navarre. His adoptive father was increasingly worried by, and afraid of, the growing revolutionary fervour in France which threatened violence and bloodshed. What Philippe found when he arrived in Navarre disturbed him greatly.

The château had been invaded by anti-aristocratic revolutionaries. The forests had been cut down. The fountains and ornamental water-falls had been smashed and the swans and deer in the park shot.

Everywhere there was uncertainty as to the future. To make the Bouillon succession absolutely clear, the increasingly beleaguered duke declared unequivocally on 25 June 1791 that, on his death, his deformed son Jacques-Leopold should become Prince Regnant; and that when Jacques died, Philippe d'Auvergne should inherit the title. However, no sooner had Philippe been confirmed in the succession than he had to leave France. Events in Paris had taken a decidedly nasty turn. The French King, Louis XVI, was virtually a prisoner of the new Legislative Assembly and everywhere the aristocrats of the *ancien régime* were under severe threat. Austria and Prussia declared war on the revolutionaries in France. Britain made threatening noises and Philippe, realising his country would soon be dragged into the conflict and considering discretion the better part of valour, returned to the safety of England.

Shortly before Louis XVI was guillotined in Paris on 21 January 1793, Duc Charles Godfrey de La Tour d'Auvergne died. In accordance with his wishes, he was buried among the poor in an Evreux cemetery. Philippe could not attend the funeral of his greatest benefactor for France and England were at war. The Revolution proceeded apace. The pathetic Jacques-Leopold, the duke's immediate successor, was deprived of his lands and imprisoned in Paris. Jacobins were in power and declared the duchy of Bouillon an independent republic. The little state was savagely attacked by the invading Austrian army and then attacked again by the French army sent to reconquer the territory. The fair town of Bouillon was sacked and the population put to the sword not once, but twice. The Directory, which was instituted to govern France in 1795, declared that the duchy would henceforth cease to be an independent state. It would be united with the rest of France. Philippe's inheritance would cease to exist.

There was little time for Philippe to bemoan his fate, however, for he was to play a very active part in the terrible wars that beset Europe. In 1794, he was given command of the aptly named *Nonsuch*, one of the oldest ships in the fleet and very, very slow. He was also given a flotilla of smaller ships and charged with the defence of the Channel Islands. He was also instructed to organise a spying network across the northern regions of France, in particular Normandy and Brittany, to keep the British Government informed as to enemy movements and enemy power. Further, he was put in charge of organising the military corps of officers raised from the royalist

Overleaf: The grand battery at Elizabeth Castle. It looks westward across St Aubin's Bay to St Aubin's Fort and keeps the gateway to Jersey secure.

refugees then flooding into Jersey and Guernsey. As if that were not enough, he had to oversee and regulate the distribution of government monies to the French immigrants.

Philippe conducted himself, as ever, with great distinction for the duration of the wars against the French Republic, carrying out his instructions to the letter. The more he assisted the French royalists, however, the more he aroused the active hatred of the Paris republicans. He thought little of it at the time.

He lived in a small castle, Hougue Bie, in the east of Jersey. La Hougue Bie is a great mound covering a neolithic tomb, or tombs, as recent excavation has shown. On top are two medieval chapels, one of which, the infamous Jerusalem Chapel, was built by Dean Mabon in the sixteenth century; in it he had performed cheap conjuring tricks to part gullible worshippers from their money. In 1760, Philippe's uncle, General James d'Auvergne, had acquired the site and 'improved' it by building a tall tower on top of the chapels. From this vantage point, almost the whole of the island and, more important, the entire length of the western coast of the Cotentin Peninsula could be observed. Uncle James passed this exotic folly on to Philippe in 1792 and d'Auvergne lived there for the first part of the French Wars.

Later, in 1802, he moved to a more comfortable residence called Bagatelle. A certain Madame Le Tour, who was no better than she should be according to the gossips, came over from France to join him in his new home. Three of Philippe's illegitimate children also lived in his house but, infuriatingly, nothing of any note is known of the mother.

Philippe was extremely busy in the 1790s during the first period of the French Wars. He was ordered to capitalise on the proximity of Jersey to Brittany in every way possible. In particular, he was to assist the royalists and guerrillas fighting government forces. It was by no means an easy task, but Philippe kept the flame of revolt very much alive in western France for many, many months. He organised a group of men who could carry letters back and forth between Jersey and Brittany, and who could also organise a supply of arms to the guerrillas, or *Chouans*. This team of brave and dedicated men were collectively known as 'La Correspondance'. They also handled the distribution of counterfeit banknotes throughout Normandy and Brittany, in the hope of undermining the French monetary system.

D'Auvergne's endeavours were frustrated by two people. First and most important, General Louis Hoche appeared on the scene to direct operations for the government. He was in command of a great army and used a stick and carrot policy to draw the sting from the *Chouans'* revolt. The second was Prigent, a trusted member of d'Auvergne's *Correspondance* organisation – and a double agent in the general's pay. This man, son of a Breton greengrocer, forewarned General Hoche of every shipment of arms and every landing of troops on Jersey. He also betrayed the whereabouts of *émigrés* fleeing to England and of fellow countrymen employed in military actions against the government armies. Betrayed and weakened by continual harassment, the *Chouans* were ready to accept the olive branch when it was offered. The central government, in return for cessation of hostilities, gave them back their own priests and gave them freedom of worship and political assembly. It released all the prisoners who had been taken in Brittany and Normandy during the protracted struggle and, most important, gave them their own elected representative in Paris. D'Auvergne continued trying to fan the insurrectionary flames but, for the time being at least, there was no possible prospect of success. There was a final battle at Pont du Lac on 25 January 1800. The government army inflicted a crushing defeat on the rump of the *Chouans*. The revolt against the Paris government was over. The *Chouan* leaders, seeing that further struggle was pointless, refused a shipment of arms sent from Jersey. Philippe could do no more. It was all over.

Peace came to all of France, now under the political and military control of that wayward genius Napoleon Bonaparte. An amnesty was granted to most of those who had previously opposed the Revolution, on condition that they would sign an oath in support of the new Constitution. As arms were laid down inside France, so outside. Governments were looking for some accord with Napoleon, some way of bringing the long and bloody wars to a close, for it was clearly pointless to go on. The French armies ruled the land. The English navy ruled the seas. It was a classic stalemate and, rather than continue with the irresolvable conflict, the warring parties came to the conference table. The Treaty of Amiens was signed in March 1802. Europe breathed a collective sigh of relief.

For Philippe, however, the ending of the French Wars was a mixed blessing. His position as Commander-in-Chief of the Channel Islands was only for the duration of the war; the post ceased to exist after Amiens. He was put on half-pay and found himself in dire financial straits. He had used much of his private money to prosecute England's cause among the French royalists in Jersey and western France. He appealed to Jersey's lieutenant-governor and even wrote to the prime minister, the Younger Pitt, pleading for some relief from the penury in which his devoted service to the crown had left him. He received but dusty answers. He was in despair.

THE CLAIMANT

In the same month of the same year that the Treaty of Amiens was signed, pitching Philippe into near destitution, something which must have raised his hopes and his spirits happened. The pathetic, mal-formed and pain-racked Jacques-Leopold of Bouillon, son of the old duke, came to the end of his sad and tormented life. By all the rights invested in him by the duke, Philippe d'Auvergne was now the legitimate ruler of the Ancient Duchy of Bouillon and Prince of Navarre. On receiving the news, he immediately adopted the full title. A new seal bore, in capital letters, the inscription SIG. PHIL. DG. DUX. BOUILLON. AD 1802.

His stepmother, Madame de Bouillon, whom the old duke had married when she was but 14 years old, had miraculously escaped execution. As an aristocrat, she had been arrested by the Jacobins, flung into a filthy dungeon in Paris and sentenced to be guillotined. The story has it that, in July 1794, she had been dragged through the streets to the place of execution in a bloodstained cart, her hair already cropped, and was kneeling with her head on the block when news of Robespierre's fall arrived together with a declaration of an amnesty for all condemned aristocrats. Her subsequent fate is unknown.

Philippe was a prince, but he had no land to rule. The old duchy had been swept away in the first flush of revolutionary fervour. All the Bouillon estates had been declared *Domaines Nationaux* and absorbed into France. What could he do? He canvassed the learned opinions of leading English lawyers and consulted friends as to the best course of action he could take. He was advised that, since France and England were at peace, he should go with all expedition to Paris and make representations directly to the French Government that they should restore all the ancient rights and lands, palaces and estates

that had belonged to the ancient and noble dukes of Bouillon. It was
universally agreed that he would have to present himself in person to
the French Government to make his appeal; nothing could be achieved
if he stayed in Jersey and tried to conduct negotiations from afar.

The task must have seemed daunting. A British naval officer, so
lately and so fiercely committed to fighting a foreign country with all
the means at his disposal, was to go to the government of that country
and ask for title and lands within it. Nevertheless, Philippe decided
to go ahead, but with all possible caution and care. The Admiralty
gave him a period of leave from duty and the Foreign Office gave him
an appropriate passport. To make assurance even more sure, the
passport was countersigned by M. Otto, the new chargé d'affaires
for the French Republic, and by the British ambassador to France,
Lord Whitworth.

So in August 1802, the would-be Prince of Bouillon set out to
make good his title. He took with him a trusted friend from Jersey,

Major Dumaresq. They were accompanied by two servants. Philippe also took a letter of introduction to Mr Merry, the British chargé d'affaires in Paris. Merry already knew of d'Auvergne's ambitions and intentions and had heard, too, that despite Philippe's role in the wars the French Government would give a sympathetic hearing to his plea. Merry had direct instructions to let the French Government know how pleased, nay delighted, the British Government would be if Philippe's title were indeed confirmed and his land restored. The thought that it would be highly advantageous to have a loyal servant of the British crown ruling a duchy in France cannot have escaped the ministers in Whitehall.

D'Auvergne and Dumaresq arrived safely in Paris on 27 August and took rooms in the Hôtel de Rome in the Rue Dominique, Faubourg St Germain. Then, like any tourists, the two men explored Paris. The Louvre was filled to overflowing with works of art, paintings, statues and tapestries, relics of antiquity brought back by Napoleon's all-conquering armies from all over the European continent. Everywhere was evidence of the bloody Revolution.

On 2 September, they saw the great Emperor Napoleon himself reviewing his troops. Philippe made his first mistake. Instead of attempting by all means to make himself known to the great man and receive a presentation, he chose to remain anonymous, as he thought, in the crowd. But he was wearing full British naval uniform at the time and was inevitably seen and recognised.

Philippe later discovered, to his chagrin, that this behaviour was considered disrespectful by Napoleon. It seems likely that, had Philippe made a direct approach to Napoleon and renounced his allegiance to Britain, he might well have regained the duchy and the estates in Normandy almost immediately. It would, of course, have been a quid pro quo settlement. Philippe would be ruler in Bouillon and Navarre, but his title would be for ever in the gift of Napoleon who could therefore count upon a lifelong supporter. It was a golden opportunity and it was missed. It may explain what followed.

According to Philippe's own account, early on the morning of

La Hougue Bie with the tower that was added by Philippe's uncle, General James d'Auvergne. Philippe lived here for some little time, but despite its imposing appearance it was very small and proved to be uncomfortable. He moved out as quickly as he could.

7 September, at 7 o'clock, he was surprised in his bed at the Hôtel de Rome by a number of ferocious-looking men, whom he found out later were police agents headed by a commissary. They set about searching his room, collecting every scrap of paper and every document and all his letters. They said they were going to take him to the Minister of Police, the thuggish Joseph Fouché. He hurriedly put on his clothes and, accompanied by eight or ten of the police agents, went by carriage to the *Bureau de la Police Générale*. He had taken the eminently sensible precaution of sending one of his servants to inform Merry of what had occurred.

On his arrival at the *Bureau,* he was put into a very small room in which 'were five or six runners [police agents] of the vilest appearance who kept going in and out every moment.' He was kept there for about an hour and then shown into the office of a M. Desmarets, secretary to Minister Fouché and an extraordinarily cruel and vindictive man.

He began to question Philippe, who interrupted him asking what motive might be ascribed to the violation of the laws of hospitality

The mighty Napoleon reviewing his troops. This is the kind of sight Philippe must have gazed upon during his unfortunate visit to Paris.

he had suffered. Desmarets replied that Minister Fouché had what he described as a prevention or prejudice against him for his work during the war, and that this was the reason for his arrest. Then, treating Philippe as if he were a captured prisoner-of-war, Desmarets tried to make him swear that Pitt had determined to wage a war of extermination in the heart of France and that he, Philippe d'Auvergne, had used his name as future Duc de Bouillon to rouse the western provinces to fight against a legitimate republican government.

Philippe refused point-blank to respond to this form of interrogation. He replied that the Treaty of Amiens had ended all hostilities between their two countries and that there was peace between England and France. There could, therefore, be no just cause for his imprisonment. He repudiated forcefully the suggestion that Pitt had waged any war of extermination, and made repeated requests to know the real reason for his detention. After about an hour, he was taken back to the small cell in which he had been first imprisoned. Here he wrote a letter to Merry. Afterwards he was given to understand that it had never reached him.

At 2 o'clock in the afternoon, he was taken for another interrogation, this time before a M. Faridel. On his way to see this gentleman he was deliberately taken through the public hall of the *Bureau* so that he could be identified by two *émigrés* who had been for some time resident in Jersey.

The interrogation followed much the same pattern as before and elicited the same answers. However, in response to repeated questions, M. Faridel let slip that he himself did not understand why Philippe was there. After about an hour of fruitless talk Philippe was returned to the cell where he had first been held.

Seven long hours later he was taken to the Temple, a grim fortress where the beautiful Marie-Antoinette and her husband, the king, had spent their last hours on Earth. It was a hideous place, scene of many a summary execution. Blood was still spattered over the walls. Philippe arrived at 11 o'clock. The order for his admission is still extant. It reads: 'The Keeper of The Temple will receive the man called La Tour d'Auvergne Bouillon, accused of spying 29 Fructidor. Fouché.' There was also a description of him at this time: 'Age 44, height five foot seven inches, hair chestnut turning grey, eyebrows ditto, forehead high and bald, eyes grey, nose short and enlarged tip, mouth medium, chin round, face round, full and highly coloured.' His details having been recorded, Philippe was taken to the apartment

O*verleaf:*
L'Archirondel Tower, with St Catherine's Bay beyond. During the nineteenth century, it was proposed to build a major harbour of refuge in the bay. The plans came to nothing.

once occupied by Madame Elizabeth, sister of the executed king.

He was led through the labyrinthine passages of the Temple and, just before he reached his own cell, he passed a dungeon in which he saw a man of terrifying appearance, dressed in rags and pale with hunger and lack of sunlight, thin, emaciated and filthy. This creature called out as Philippe passed, '*Quoi donc une autre victime est-ce que cela ne finira jamais?*' (What, another victim, will this never end?).

The police agents had not taken Philippe's purse and he was able to bribe his gaoler to bring him some food and drink – cold fowl, bread and a bottle of red wine – the first he had had that day. The gaoler proved to be a friendly fellow and had some conversation with the luckless Jerseyman, who asked him who the wretch was he had just seen in the dungeon. '*C'est un mouton,*' (lamb) the gaoler replied conspiratorially. '*Fermer bien votre porte*' (Shut your trap). Philippe did not understand.

That night he slept not at all. His bedding was filthy and lice-ridden, so he spent the hours pacing up and down trying to think of the reason for his arrest. The only one that sprang to mind was that the vindictive Fouché, well aware of the major role Philippe had played in the uprising and insurrections in the west of France, was seeking revenge.

The infamous Temple in Paris, where Philippe was incarcerated. Revolutionary justice had been dispensed here with unforgiving and bloody ferocity.

On the morning of 8 September, while taking exercise in the tiny garden, Philippe fell in with a M. Fanche, imprisoned for publishing anti-government literature. In the course of their conversation, Philippe told him about the prisoner he had seen and inquired what was meant by calling someone a *mouton*. Fanche told him that a *mouton* was not a real prisoner at all, but an *agent provocateur* in police pay. Gaunt, filthy and thin, he would gain the sympathy and trust of real prisoners. Whatever damning remarks they made against ministers, or the government in general, would be reported to the police and used in evidence against them. Philippe was so angered by this revelation that, by a combination of bullying and bribery, he had the *mouton* removed from his part of the Temple.

There was still no news of his release. By liberal use of his money, he managed to get some decent bedding and a quantity of food. Suddenly, at 3 o'clock in the afternoon of his third day of captivity, the door to his prison was flung open and Major Dumaresq was ushered in. He too had been arrested and, just like Philippe, had no idea why.

Meanwhile Merry was mightily exercised to secure their release. He tried to approach Fouché, but was fobbed off by underlings who offered neither excuse nor explanation for the imprisonment. In desperation, Merry made a formal application for their release to the most powerful man in France after Napoleon: the Foreign Minister, Talleyrand. No answer came. The days passed by.

At last, on 12 September, the two Jerseymen were allowed their freedom – but only after Philippe had another interview with M. Desmarets, who offered him a deal. If Philippe told him all he knew of the British Government's policies and intentions, the duchy of Bouillon and all the estates, including the château of Navarre, would be his. It was a tempting offer. He was, after all, a French nobleman by adoption; might his first loyalty and obedience thus be to France and not to the British crown?

Philippe d'Auvergne's response was unequivocal and immediate. His first loyalty, he averred, continued to be to the British crown. He would not inform on the activities or intentions of the British Government. He would not enter into any correspondence, of whatever kind, with M. Fouché.

That was that. He was ordered to leave France forthwith, which he duly did, and arrived back in Jersey on 27 September. His ambition should, perhaps, have been made of less noble stuff. For it is certain

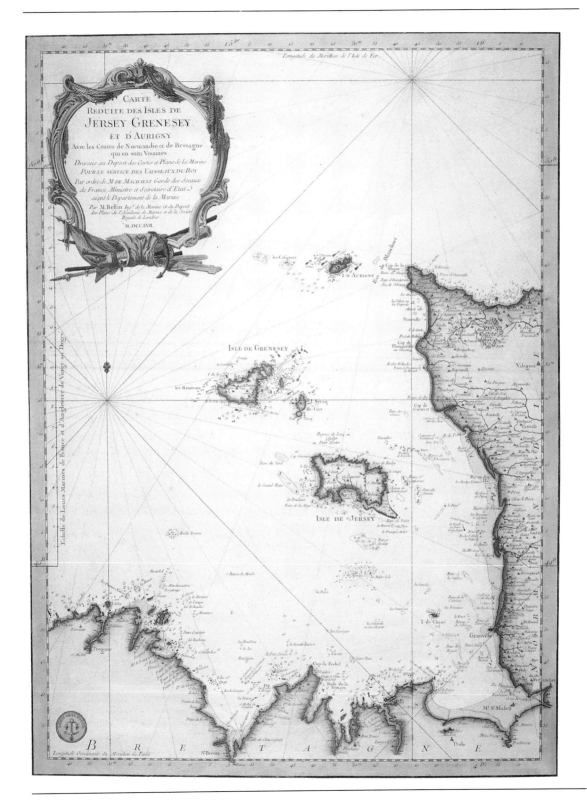

that he was now as far away from realising his dreams as he had ever been. He rested in Jersey for a few days, recovering from the indignities and hardship of his visit to Paris. He then travelled to London where, by dint of ceaseless lobbying, he managed to get his case discussed in Parliament by the foremost statesmen of the day. No less a person than Charles Fox argued vehemently that the treatment meted out to an authorised British officer by the French was sufficient ground to re-open the war. The Government, however, was in no hurry to renew hostilities, whatever the insult offered to Philippe. Lord Liverpool voiced the official line: 'It must be confirmed that Captain d'Auvergne was the person who carried on our correspondence with our friends in France and is charged by the French Government with still giving protection in his island to those who fly from the neighbouring French coast.' In other words, the French Government, believing Philippe to be a spy, had acted quite properly. Philippe's arrest, imprisonment and abrupt deportation was unfortunate, but certainly excusable. In no way did the French action constitute a *casus belli*.

Philippe d'Auvergne returned to Jersey a defeated man. He was a naval officer on half-pay, and very poor. But hope was to come from an unexpected quarter and in an unexpected way.

Napoleon Bonaparte broke the Treaty of Amiens in 1803. The armies of France were on the march again. Europe was at war. This was good news for Philippe, who was restored, on his old pay, to his old position as Commander-in-Chief of the Channel Islands. His brief was as before: to defend the islands from attack and also re-establish, as best he could, the *Correspondance*.

Philippe, who now insisted on being called Prince of Bouillon, brought all his considerable expertise to bear in executing his instructions, and was promoted to admiral in 1809. He was, however, subject to bouts of worry and depression for the very good reason that he saw how contradictory were his actions and ambitions. He wanted to be a French nobleman, and here he was fighting Frenchmen who were under the command of the very person who might have made him such. While Napoleon ruled, Philippe could not succeed in Bouillon. These morbid introspective periods were not helped by his recurrent ill health, a legacy of his enforced sojourn on Trinidad. At other times he could be funny, witty and vibrant, cracking jokes and telling stories of foreign fields in that thick Jersey accent that came so strangely from the mouth of a British admiral.

Map that shows Jersey's proximity to Brittany – and how easy it was for Philippe to organise the 'Correspondance'.

Philippe succeeded all too well in organising resistance to Bonaparte's rule. As Napoleon himself wrote in the official newspaper, the *Moniteur*: 'The government of His Britannic Majesty permits, nay authorises, hundreds of brigands, assassins, fire bugs to find refuge in Jersey, whence they slip back into France to commit further crime.' The great emperor was greatly angered. Again from the *Moniteur*: 'No! France can tolerate no longer this nest of brigands and assassins. Europe must be purged from the vermin. Jersey is England's disgrace.'

Napoleon was so incensed by d'Auvergne's activities that he took vigorous steps, with considerable success, to suppress the uprisings Philippe organised in Brittany and Normandy.

Napoleon had no reason on Earth to love Philippe. He must have taken a special pleasure in disposing, among his own family, of the estates that Philippe wanted for himself and thought of as his own. The emperor gave the great Château de Navarre, still splendid despite a decade of deprivation and destruction, to his divorced wife, the Empress Josephine. (She did not enjoy herself there one little bit, finding the palace cold and boring.) The duchy of Bouillon, he gave to his nephew, the son of Prince Eugène Napoleon. Philippe could see no hope of claiming his inheritance. Everywhere Napoleon was triumphant and seemingly invincible. England alone held out.

Then, as another dictator was to do 130 years later, Napoleon turned towards the east and took on the might of Russia. He was defeated and forced into ignominious retreat by the Russian armies. In the deep and unforgiving winter of 1812, he lost three-quarters of a million men. It signalled the beginning of the end.

The countries of Europe, sensing their advantage, rallied to destroy once and for all the over-ambitious First Consul of France. The scent of death was in the air. An alliance, as mighty as it was rare, of Russia, Austria, Prussia, Sweden and Britain relentlessly harried and chased the French armies across Europe. Bonaparte, his back against a very high wall, summoned up all his military genius and achieved many spectacular victories. But he was always fighting a rearguard action. He may have won several battles, and that brilliantly, but he was losing the war.

At Leipzig, Napoleon suffered a terrible defeat. His armies, routed, fled for their lives. The allies swept irresistibly over the French frontiers and into Paris. By 4 April 1814 it was all over. The greatest general the modern world has ever known relinquished his hold on power by signing a formal abdication. He was banished to the tiny island of Elba.

In the bag and baggage of the allies, came the weak-willed, gouty, sagging, sensualist, Louis XVIII. This caricature of royalty was duly placed upon the French throne. With that act, it seemed as if the old order had been at last restored, more or less intact. Now was the moment of Philippe d'Auvergne's greatest hope. The king was bound to restore all the ducal rights and princedoms, all the traditional customs and principles of succession that had existed before the madness of revolution had swept them away. Louis' own legitimacy as sovereign depended on such a restoration. Might he not restore the Ancient Duchy of Bouillon and the Château de Navarre to Philippe? Indeed he might. The more so because, throughout the duration of the Revolution, Philippe had mercilessly harried and attacked republican armies without respite. He had given shelter and political refuge to hard-pressed royalists fleeing for their lives out of France. Moreover, he had supplied, with unremitting diligence, all the guerrilla groups in western France – often at great danger to himself. Philippe d'Auvergne had served the cause of French royalism as well as he had served the British crown, for it was the same service and the same cause. As much as Napoleon hated Philippe d'Auvergne, Louis had reason to love him.

His head high, his thoughts all of his inheritance at last, Philippe rushed to Paris. The French king met him cordially and intimated that he supported his claims to Bouillon and Navarre. Philippe also had a more powerful friend in the shape of the Duke of Wellington, ostensibly the British ambassador to the French court but, in reality, wielding considerably more power than his title suggested. This great man, too, supported the Jerseyman's claim.

Philippe d'Auvergne, now 60 years old, Duke Regnant of Bouillon, Prince of Navarre, as he liked to call himself, must have considered that the long, long years of waiting were over. He looked forward to spending the rest of his life in his duchy, in full possession of great lands and palaces, a French lord of the first rank. Of course, there would be much to do. Bouillon had been horribly pillaged and wrecked by successive invading armies. Houses had been torn down, the old Court House had been burnt, farms had been left untended and the great castle itself had been partially destroyed. The people were poor and famished. The Château de Navarre, too, was in a desperate state of disrepair. Trees had been thoughtlessly hacked

Overleaf: Part of the rugged coastline along the northern coast towards Sorel Point. It is a natural defence against an enemy.

down, the grounds were flooded with water from the smashed ornamental fountains and waterfalls. A foetid swamp surrounded the palace. More important, many of the exquisite statues inside had been broken up and the art treasures stolen. It would take years to restore the damage. But what matter? From the Arctic to the South Atlantic, from the Channel Islands to India, Philippe d'Auvergne had spent a lifetime confronting fearful challenges. He had not failed in one of them.

So certain was he of success that, on his own authority, he set up a provisional government in the duchy while the details of his restoration were being worked out by the Congress of Vienna. He nominated his successor to the title Duc de Bouillon: the Duc de Tremouille-Tarente, grandson of an aunt of the old duke. He issued orders through the provisional government that his oppressed people should no longer have to pay taxes on certain items such as salt and tobacco. He had coins struck, with his image on one side and the duchy's arms on the other. He called up the great number of young men who formed Bouillon's militia and, from his own purse, provided them with handsome uniforms.

A final act to seal Philippe's succession took place on 10 January 1815. The members of the provisional government and all the important members of Bouillon society assembled and took the following solemn oath: 'We swear before God to give loyal obedience to his most Serene Highness Prince Philippe d'Auvergne the Duke Regnant and his Most Serene Highness the Prince of Tremouille-Tarente the Prince's successor, to give no countenance to any party or plot that may be formed against them and if we hear that anything is afoot that is prejudicial to their interests, we will at once reveal it.'

All his Serene Highness the Duc de Bouillon had to do was wait for the final, and inevitable, ratification of his claims by a Congress engaged in the arduous, and exquisitely sensitive, work of redrawing the map of Europe after Bonaparte. A special committee was formed to discuss, and decide on, the future of the duchy.

The problem facing the committee is easily summarised. The grand strategy of the Congress was to create a strong buffer state lying between eastern France and the rest of Europe, the better to prevent a repetition of the recent wars. To this end, it was proposed to join together Belgium and Holland to form a new kingdom: The Netherlands. Bouillon lay in the very middle of the proposed kingdom. It made little sense politically, economically or strategically to allow a small, independent, sovereign state to continue to exist at the very heart of the new creation. A thorny problem indeed.

It was not made any easier by the sudden appearance of another claimant to the Bouillon inheritance: Prince Charles de Rohan, a grandson of a stepsister of the old Duc de Bouillon. It was a distant claim and it was stoutly opposed by the people of the duchy themselves. The chancellor of the duchy stated that any challenge or objection to the old duke's will creating Philippe his legal heir should have been made in the year of the signing, but that Charles de Rohan had waited more than 20 years to protest. In law, it was now too late to object. Philippe remained confident that the committee's final decision would be in his favour.

The final judgement read:

———————————————— ● ————————————————

His Majesty the King of the Netherlands, shall possess in perpetuity for himself and his successors in full and entire sovereignty the Duchy of Bouillon. Of certain claimants to the Duchy who have appeared the one who can legally prove his right shall possess under the sovereignty of the King of the Netherlands the land held by the late Duke. Arbitrators shall be nominated one by each of the claimants and three others by the courts of Austria, Prussia and Sardinia as soon as the state of the war permits. Their decision shall be final.

———————————————— ● ————————————————

It was heartrending, but Philippe scarcely had time to reflect on his shattered hopes. Napoleon broke free from Elba and commenced a triumphal march through France. The people flocked to him. Napoleon was *la France*, he was *la gloire*, far more than was the politically impotent Louis XVIII. Better to have a man they knew and loved to decide their fate than a lot of anonymous foreigners cutting up their country between banquets and balls in Vienna. Napoleon's enterprise was, in truth, desperate. The clock could not be turned back. He was defeated at Waterloo on 18 June 1815. The Congress resumed the delicate task of deciding who owned what.

Philippe's hopes revived. He seemed to believe that somehow, sometime, the committee, on the orders of the Congress in full session, would reverse its decision. In that expectation, and in direct contravention of the committee's ruling, he travelled to the duchy and tried to establish himself as ruler. The Dutch ambassador had to

*O*verleaf: One of Jersey's most spectacular views: Elizabeth Castle from West Mount. St Helier's little chapel can be seen atop the rock to the left before the breakwater.

threaten him with military force if he did not give up his occupation. There was no possible way to resist. Philippe knew that his days as sovereign duke were numbered; he could not hope to resist the combined power of all the European nations that would be ranged against him. Bitterly admitting defeat, he at last left the duchy he had so long hoped to make his final home. It was not quite the end.

If he had irrevocably lost any claim to sovereignty in Bouillon, there was still the question of the private lands, palaces, castles and estates belonging to the old duke. If Philippe were confirmed as the true and rightful heir, he could still be a rich and powerful man.

On the instructions of the committee of the Congress of Vienna, arbitrators were appointed and met in the summer of 1815 at Leipzig. With more than a passing interest in their proceedings, Philippe himself took up residence in that city to observe and to hope. In the end there were just two claimants to the old duke's rich estates: Prince Charles de Rohan and Philippe d'Auvergne.

Philippe was again confident that the arbitrators would find in his favour and, again, his confidence was ill-founded. After a protracted debate, they found for Prince Charles de Rohan on the grounds that a blood relative had more right to inherit than someone whose only claim rested on adoption. Philippe d'Auvergne's claim was declared null and void. Charles de Rohan received handsome compensation from the Dutch Government for his loss of sovereignty, and became the acknowledged Duc de Bouillon with possession of all the private estates belonging to that title.

Philippe got nothing. He had nothing. All his small fortune had been spent pursuing his claims to the duchy. He had borrowed substantial sums of money to pay for his extended stay in France and for the uniforms of the duchy troops, the coins he had minted and the many lawyers he had consulted. He had pawned his life and his fortune to pursue his dream of nobility. He had failed. He fell from prince to pauper and his legion creditors came banging on his door.

The arbitrators' decision ended his life. He travelled to London a few weeks after his world had been utterly destroyed, an old and sick man. There he found no friend, despite his long, devoted service to his country. On 18 September 1815, at the Homes Hotel in Parliament Street, the great and tragic Jerseyman died.

He was buried in a little church in the shadow of Westminster Abbey. A small marble tablet was erected to his memory, its modesty at odds with the greatness of his ambition.

4

THE WATERSHED YEARS

*T*he nineteenth century was a time of tremendous change in this small island. Many of the buldings and monuments which are now an integral part of Jersey's image were constructed during these years. It is, of course, true, as it always was, that most of these structures were erected because of the threat of war. It was the very real fear that Jersey would be invaded by Napoleonic forces that prompted the construction of Fort Regent on Town Hill. The work began in 1806 and was completed in 1814, the year that Bonaparte was exiled to Elba. This vast construction, designed by Major (later Lieutenant-General) John Hambly Humfrey, remains to this day one of Europe's finest examples of a nineteenth-century military fort.

At the same time Sir George Don, Lieutenant-Governor of Jersey from 1806 to 1814, was busy building more defensive works all around the coastline. He also had new roads constructed to facilitate the quicker movement of troops around the island. The local farmers were none too pleased but Don finally achieved his goal. He built fine roads, particularly the one from St Aubin to St Helier. The two towns had previously been joined only by the beach, and that only when the tide was low. Sir George constructed twenty major roads round the island and his work still remains at the core of Jersey's infrastructure.

The threat of Bonaparte passed. Great changes were about to occur. At the beginning of the century, the island was inhabited mostly by Jersey-born people, all of whom spoke the Jersey patois. It is true that English was widely spoken and understood, but it was very much a second language. Jersey French was spoken in the streets, in the fields, in the States and in the churches.

The island folk worked the land or the sea. Some did both. Cider was still the main produce of Jersey. In 1840, more than 330 000 gallons were exported to England. The great granite cider presses can still be seen today in many farms, usually filled with flowers rather

Jersey's native architecture as expressed in Jersey granite (*above and right*). Simple and functional, but distinctive and beautiful, it has largely been superseded by newer and more vulgar styles that can be seen along St Aubin's Bay and the eastern coast towards Gorey. The price of a certain type of progress!

than apples. There was also cereal cultivation and cattle farming, although Jersey had to wait a little longer for the Jersey cow, the greatest invention of that truly remarkable Jerseyman, Sir John Le Couteur. Then there were the great oyster beds in Grouville Bay, with thousands of men and women employed in the business of dredging and packing. Unfortunately, the beds were ruined by over-farming and the industry went into decline. It has recently been revived, however, by the Royal Bay Oyster Company. They produce some of the tastiest shellfish I have ever eaten and business is thriving. Jersey, then as now, had a large fishing fleet and some of the vessels were used to smuggle tobacco and spirits from France to mainland England. Smuggling still goes on, but these days the contraband is not so much liquor and tobacco as drugs such as cannabis and, more seriously, heroin.

The architecture of the island was individual and distinctive. The houses built of the local pink granite were, and those that remain still are, models of simplicity and beauty. They were functional and elegant and, because they were built from indigenous materials, they melded into the surrounding countryside in a very pleasing manner.

Life on the island at the start of the nineteenth century was varied, vibrant and colourful and the people were quite prosperous. It was a way of life separate from, and very different to, life on mainland Britain. All this was to change.

Early in the century, the protracted wars with France were over. The huge armies were disbanded and some 5000 ex-officers on their pensions headed for this beautiful island. They and their families made Jersey their home and, in so doing, changed the nature of island society for ever. At first, these immigrants formed a society within a society. They spoke a different language and had different interests to the islanders. Gradually, however, they made their presence more and more felt, their voices more and more heard, until the dominant style in island life was definitely English. It was then, in those 20 years after Waterloo, that the process of Anglicisation was begun. It has continued to this present day. Many fear that it will go on and on until everything that made Jersey unique and different disappears into the history books. They have good reason to be so afraid.

The English brought with them their own mainland notions, often very much at variance with those of the locals. Their houses, for example, were not built after the simple Jersey style but in the English styles: Regency and then Victorian. Some of this architecture, such as Royal Crescent in Don Street, was quite pleasant. The crescent originally had as its centrepiece a neo-classical theatre, which was unfortunately burned down. It was replaced by the New Bible Christian Church. This building was demolished in 1967 and there is now an ugly gap where the centrepiece of the crescent should be. There are uglier sights, many of them in St Helier which expanded rapidly during these years. The Masonic Temple at the end of Beresford Street is an example. It was built in 1864 by Thomas Gallichan. At that time the entire membership of the five island masonic lodges did not exceed 120 men. The building is big enough for 2000. It is, as C. E. B. Brett remarks in his 1977 survey of St Helier buildings, an extraordinary, heavy and forbidding, Corinthian stucco monster. Many other examples of such awesome pretension can be found all around the island, particularly in St Ouen and St John.

Latterly all kinds of buildings – houses, hotels, offices and leisure centres – have been erected with seemingly very little or no regard for the appearance or size of the island. Huge blocks of luxury flats, far too large for such a small place, have appeared in Grouville along the Route de la Haule and on the Victor Hugo site. Such places would not be out of place in Marbella or Monte Carlo, but they are overpowering on this small island. It is all part of the movement, begun 150 years ago, to make Jersey more English than England.

That movement really got into its stride during Victoria's long reign. English currency was adopted. A great number of English-language newspapers began to appear on the streets. A telegraph system was installed between the English mainland and Jersey. Money from England poured in to help build a new railway from St Helier to St Aubin and Gorey. Representatives of the English community pressed for political reform along English lines. This was partially achieved in 1856, when elected deputies took their seats in the States for the first time. Jersey was being bound ever more closely to Britain.

The visit of Queen Victoria in 1846 confirmed this new relationship. It was an extraordinary occasion, the first time that a reigning British monarch had stepped on to Jersey soil. Sir John Le Couteur, Victoria's aide-de-camp, was as excited by the prospect as the rest of Jersey and anxious that everything should go smoothly. It would have helped if Victoria and the Prince Albert had let the people of Jersey know what they intended to do, or even the precise time they meant to arrive on the island. Unfortunately for Sir John, royal itineraries were not planned as far in advance, and in such meticulous

Sir John Le Couteur, undoubtedly the greatest Jerseyman of the last century. His interests were many and his achievements considerable. The most notable was his creation of the Jersey cow.

detail, as now. Indeed, 4 days before the queen arrived Sir John was writing to her naval aide-de-camp begging him for information concerning the visit. The ADC replied that Her Majesty was leaving the mainland within the next 2 days, but that he was not yet absolutely certain where she was going.

Sir John took no chances. He played safe and made the correct assumption that the queen would come to Jersey. What precisely she would want to do when she got there, where precisely she would want to stay – if indeed she was going to stay any length of time at all – he knew not. The bailiff, Sir John de Veulle, and he simply prepared for every eventuality. The sickly Sir Edward Gibbs, lieutenant-governor, gave orders for a look-out to be posted at La

Moye and Noirmont with instructions to relay news of the queen's imminent arrival to Elizabeth Castle as fast as they could, if and when the royal squadron was observed. Two guns would then be fired from the castle and a right royal greeting for a right royal lady would be instantly prepared.

All was expectancy, the ladies endlessly worrying about what to wear, the boys in the militia polishing up their buttons and boots, the Jersey folk in every parish hanging out decorations in the streets and lanes or building fantastic ornamental arches across the roads on the off-chance that the queen might come their way. Sir John ordered a gun to be fired over the heads of the horses that were to draw Victoria's carriage, to see whether they would become restive, or even bolt, from the noise of a royal procession. The animals behaved perfectly.

On a perfect late summer evening, 2 September, the royal squadron hove into view round Noirmont Point. Rockets were let off, a salute was fired from Elizabeth Castle, the islanders crowded to St Helier. The royal yacht was accompanied by three other steamers: the *Garland*, the *Fairy* and the *Black Eagle*. Sir John, resplendent in his red uniform, the bailiff and the lieutenant-governor's deputy (Sir Edward was ill) rode out to greet Her Majesty and the Prince Albert. Prince Albert appeared first. Sir John de Veulle, the bailiff, handed him a prepared itinerary for the next day and Albert took it to the queen below decks. On his re-emergence he enquired as to the best time to land in Jersey. On being told the state of the tides, it was decided that Queen Victoria, the first monarch to step voluntarily on to island soil since time beyond record, would commence her visit at 11 o'clock the following morning.

Sir John made a plea for Victoria to visit the western parishes as they had been to such a great deal of trouble to prepare for her. Albert, however, decided that such a long journey would tire his wife too much and it was agreed that the queen would instead travel up the eastern parishes to visit Mont Orgueil Castle, which was quaintly described as a 'beautiful old castle built by the Romans'. All the details settled, the diminutive queen came on deck to greet the knights of Jersey in person. She graciously remarked how much she was looking forward to seeing such a beautiful island.

Despite all the preparations and planning, there was a certain amount of panic on the great day. Sir John himself spent a restless night and was up at 4.30 a.m. He dressed with extra care and at 9 o'clock addressed the regiment of militia assembled at the Black Rocks. He recorded in his diary that he urged them to be, 'Steady as rocks while the queen passed them'. Thousands upon thousands of people were already lining the streets. The harbour itself was black with people. Sir John organised the horses which were to pull the royal carriage and then hurried to the landing-stage where the queen and Prince Albert would arrive.

Everything was in uproar. The ladies, perspiring in their finery for it was an exceedingly hot day, were not at all sure where they should stand, how they should stand or, indeed, what they should say to the queen. The assembled members of the States were in no better case as to the protocol of the occasion. Should they be presented individually? If so, who would decide in what order? Who would present the loyal addresses and how would they be presented? Sir John, besieged on all sides by such questions, hurriedly introduced some order into the assembled company, giving everyone strict instructions as how to behave when Her Majesty came among them. He then rushed down the steps to greet the queen and Prince Albert. After being assured that the landing box, covered with a crimson cloth and a rich rug, was safe Victoria 'biting her lip with emotion at the thundering cheers of 20 000 voices' (John Le Couteur) stepped on to Jersey soil.

Sir John presented the ladies first: the bailiff's wife, Lady de Veulle, Mary le Maistre, daughter of the Seigneur of St Ouen and, with a special feeling of delight, his own daughter, Harriet Le Couteur. The queen then sat back under an awning while the loyal addresses were presented, first by the bailiff and then by Colonel Le Breton for the Militia. It was all going very well, although a certain Mr Le Seur, who was to present a loyal address for the parish of St Helier, either forgot or took fright, but in any event had disappeared when his presentation was due. It was a minor hiccup.

Sir John conducted Queen Victoria towards her carriage. She appeared amazed at the great number of people that thronged to see her. All up the Mont de Ville and down the Pier Road, people were everywhere. In the harbour they were crowded into boats and clinging to masts and yard-arms to get a better view. The young queen, complete with parasol, climbed into the carriage beside Albert and the royal progress began through the crowded streets of St Helier. The town was lavishly and festively decorated with flowers and arches. To the Royal Square they went. Sir John, tall and distinguished if a little hot, rode his charger a little to the queen's right and kept Her Majesty informed as to points of interest along the way: the poor 'charity' children lined up to wave; the place where Major Peirson had laid down his life in 1781, bravely defending Jersey against the French; the gilded statue of George II; and the gaily dressed French women in their national costumes.

As they left the Royal Square and were passing St Mark's Church, the queen noticed that the States members, who were on foot behind the royal carriage, were having more than a little difficulty in keeping up with their sovereign. She told Sir John to tell them that they were relieved of their duty. The members came gratefully to rest by the side of the road and Victoria continued her journey to Mont Orgueil. In those days it was a very countrified journey with very few houses and many, many more trees than now. 'What a pretty, rich country this is. So quiet,' said Victoria.

At Mont Orgueil the queen climbed up to the Grand Battery and looked out over the Channel through her telescope. Sir John was all attention. They discussed plans to have a harbour of refuge in Jersey and the argument that was raging as to the best site for it: St Catherine,

A romantic view of Mont Orgueil Castle and harbour, which Queen Victoria visited in 1846. The name means 'Mount Pride'.

Bouley Bay or, Wellington's preferred site, Noirmont. They then discussed the local language, the queen remarking how she was very much in favour of those 'old attachments to language'.

St Helier was still packed with happy people when the royal couple returned from Gorey. The good Jersey folk cheered the queen down the streets, cheered her to the harbour, on to her barge and all the way back to the royal squadron.

The visit had lasted only 3 hours but its political significance was incalculable. Streets and crescents were named after her, statues and buildings were erected in her honour – of varying quality, it must be said. The statue *érigé par le peuple* now standing behind the toilets in the park by the Grand Hotel is scarcely a success. Brett describes it as a 'cross between Widow Twankey and the White Queen in *Alice in Wonderland*.' Victoria College, however, is a fine old building of the kind John Betjeman would have loved. It was built on the high ground to the east of St Helier and has proved to be a very fine school.

Queen Victoria saw it on her second visit to the island 13 years later, in August 1859. This was an embarrassing occasion for the island authorities, although in all honesty they could not be blamed

The departure of Queen Victoria from Jersey in 1846. Her visit marked the beginning of a process of determined Anglicisation that has lasted to the present day.

for the lack of preparation. Victoria gave absolutely no notice of her intention to visit the island and, as a result, everyone was utterly unprepared to provide a proper welcome for her. The queen had come on the sudden advice of Prince Albert. He was anxious because she was melancholic and depressed by one of the perennial disputes she insisted on having with her Cabinet. A visit to Jersey would perhaps cheer her up, he thought.

The occasion was not a resounding success. In fact, it was near chaos. There were no militia men to line the queen's way and keep people at bay as she rode through St Helier *en route* for Victoria College. Consequently, the crowds came too close and distressed her with their riotous behaviour, pressing round the royal carriage, the women pelting her with flowers. She finally arrived, somewhat distraught, at the college. No proper preparation had been made there for her reception.

So far, the queen's second visit to the island was not going at all well. She wanted to return to the yacht, but had to wait half an hour for the tide. However, Sir John Le Couteur persuaded her to come ashore again in the late afternoon. Diplomatic and wise as ever, he recognised Her Majesty's need for a little peace and quiet as far as possible from the public gaze. He took her in his carriage up St Peter's valley, the most beautiful of the beautiful island valleys, through the wooded and dappled northern parishes to St Catherine's. As they had done 13 years before, they must once more have discussed harbours of refuge; St Catherine's Breakwater had been completed by this time, at no little cost and for no good purpose. It seems that the queen enjoyed this respite from the public round. The burdened lady was much happier when she left from St Catherine's that evening than when she first arrived in St Helier.

It was on this occasion, on her visit to Victoria College, that the Dean of Jersey, William Corbet Le Breton, handed the great queen a quill pen with which to sign the visitors' book. The pen would not write. The queen was not pleased. She let it fall from her fingers and, looking straight ahead, waited with ill-concealed annoyance for a replacement. The dean told his daughter of this embarrassing experience, and she remembered it clearly when it was her turn to be introduced to Queen Victoria. Her name was Lillie Langtry.

5

THE JERSEY LILY
Lillie Langtry
(1853–1929)

You are the most exasperating subject I have ever painted. You look just beautiful for about fifty-five out of sixty minutes but for five in every hour you are amazing. Sir John Millais on Lillie Langtry.

Indeed she was amazing. Ruthless, ambitious, gold-digging, the most remarkable woman Jersey has ever produced. Loved by kings and poets, gangsters and charlatans, she was the scandal and the glory of the age. It was her beauty that was her fortune, a beauty captured most perfectly by Sir John Millais in the portrait that hangs on the wall in the Langtry room at *La Société Jersiaise* in St Helier. She had a fine face and long dark hair, but it was her complexion that admirers remarked on most. 'Like a peach,' the Countess of Warwick wrote. 'How can words convey the vitality, the glow, the amazing charm that made this fascinating woman the centre of any group she entered?' Oscar Wilde, no mean judge of beauty, remarked, 'I would rather have discovered Lillie Langtry than America.' Many would have agreed with him.

Lillie was born Emily Charlotte Le Breton in the Old Rectory in St Saviour in Jersey. Her father was William Corbet Le Breton, Dean of Jersey. Her mother, Emily, had already borne him five sons and was to bear him one more. Naturally enough, Lillie was a tomboy joining with her brothers in most of their escapades. They draped sheets over their heads and stood on stilts, appearing from behind gravestones to astonish and frighten the life out of passers-by. Or fastened lengths of string across driveways to lift off ladies' bonnets.

Right: Lillie's signature scratched on to a window-pane at the Old Rectory in St Saviour. This is where she spent her carefree childhood days.

Overleaf: The Old Rectory, St Saviour, which still stands. It was the scene of many a youthful escapade – and a fine example of Jersey vernacular architecture.

They also had a jolly time stealing their neighbours' door knockers.

Lillie may have been a tomboy, but by the time she was fourteen she was certainly very pretty. Sir John Le Couteur recounts several times meeting Mrs Le Breton with her beautiful daughter. She was pretty enough to turn the head of a young officer of the island garrison, Lieutenant Arthur Longley, son of the Archbishop of Canterbury. He saw Lillie galloping her horse through the sea and along the sands of St Aubin's Bay and, as many, many men were to do, fell helplessly and hopelessly in love with her. He approached the dean for permission to marry his daughter. The dean gravely informed him that she was still a schoolgirl who could not possibly contemplate marriage. The poor lieutenant, somewhat abashed, left the rectory a sadder and a wiser man. Shortly after, he left the island for good.

Lillie grew ever more beautiful and, as it happened, she fell in love. She was seventeen, he was a year younger. Details of their meeting and their courtship are few and far between. Lillie herself makes no mention of the affair in her somewhat reticent auto-biography, *The Days I Knew*, and it is easy to see why. The boy was, in fact, the son of Lillie's father – the result of an illicit liaison between the dean and a local woman. To prevent the association of his daughter and son developing, he had to tell Lillie the truth. The shock must have been considerable for she had always regarded her father with great respect, devotion and admiration. She recalled later that he was a remarkably handsome man and that he was widely admired for his geniality and charm. Indeed, prints of the time show a fine,

tall man with a granite jaw and piercing eyes. Lillie was convinced he could have cut a fine figure on the professional stage. As it was, he cut a much shabbier one in Jersey society. His womanising over the years became too much to bear and, in 1880, he was required to leave the island. He ended his days, deserted by his wife, in the poor London parish of Kennington. He died in February 1888, still nominally Dean of Jersey but with only £5 to his name. There is no mention of this fall from grace in Lillie's autobiography, although she admitted to friends that her father's licentiousness was a liability. Her own, of course, she turned into an asset. The wretched fellow was buried in St Saviour's churchyard, where Lillie was to find her final resting-place some 40 years later.

To compensate Lillie for the trauma of falling in love with her half-brother, her mother took her on a visit to London. After the quiet and rather conservative social life of Jersey, London was a revelation and, although no glittering entry into high society could be effected at that time, Lillie was nevertheless impressed with what she saw. It is more than likely that her great ambition one day to take the capital by storm was born during this visit. Everyone of consequence she met told her she was beautiful, and Lord Ranelagh, an old roué and friend from Jersey, told her she should try for a season in London where he thought it was certain she would have a great success. We may take it that the young Lillie was not unimpressed by such advice.

On 19 November 1872, Edward Langtry, chubby, ineffectual, round-shouldered, weak-chinned and curiously plain, came sailing into Jersey in his 80-foot luxury yacht the *Red Gauntlet*. Lillie said later, 'To become the mistress of the yacht, I married the owner.' She was very impressed by Langtry's great wealth. His grandfather had been the richest shipowner in Belfast.

Edward's first wife, Jane Frances Price, had died tragically young at 20 years old of tuberculosis. Lillie's brother William was to marry Jane's sister and Edward had come to attend the wedding. Lillie was one of the bridesmaids. After the ceremony, Edward threw a ball in honour of the happy couple at the Jersey yacht club. Lillie was dazzled beyond expression by the opulence of the show. Such open-handed generosity spoke volumes to her. Seven days later, Edward Langtry asked for her hand in marriage. The Le Breton family opposed the union. Mrs Le Breton, very sensible of her daughter's outstanding charms, thought she should have a season in London in the hope of

Lillie, or Emily as she then was, her brother, mother and father pose somewhat stiffly for a photograph. The look of virtuous propriety on the face of her father belies the truth. He became known as the 'Dirty Dean'.

catching an even bigger fish. The dean thought Lillie still too young for marriage. Nevertheless, she finally got her way and on the morning of 9 March 1874 was married to Edward by her father.

Lillie Langtry had arrived. Edward, however, was not quite the man she thought him to be. Indeed, the Le Bretons privately doubted that the marriage was ever consummated. Truth to tell, Lillie found him rather dull and shy of the company she craved. Life became pretty boring as she sailed in Edward's various yachts, getting wet, cold and becalmed in all senses of the word. London seemed light years away.

The next year she fell very seriously ill with typhoid fever and was confined to Edward's Southampton house, Cliff Lodge. A doctor advised that a change of air was needed. Lillie suggested that they remove to London and persuaded the doctor to her opinion. And so to London they finally went, despite Edward's well-founded misgivings. However, the couple had hardly settled into Brown's Hotel in Piccadilly, and Lillie had scarcely begun casting about for an entrée into high society, than there came the awful news that one of her brothers, Reggie, had died. He had been crushed to death by a horse. Her social ambitions tragically thwarted, she and her husband took an interminable journey back to Jersey.

Edward took the manor house where Lillie's ancestors, the seigneurs of Noirmont, had once lived, but even here she quickly grew depressed and unwell. She had, in truth, outgrown Jersey. She wanted London; she had got only as far as Southampton. The medical profession in the shape of the local doctor came to aid her ambition once more, advising the Langtrys to move to the metropolis. The compliant Edward duly took his wife to the capital. This time she was to stay.

Lillie managed to join the London glitterati through an extremely fortunate and fortuitous meeting. She and her husband were returning from a visit to the Royal Aquarium, a sort of circus in Westminster that featured all kinds of freak shows and novelty acts, when suddenly she saw Lord Ranelagh strolling towards them through the crowds. She had been very friendly with his two daughters in Jersey, and possibly more than friendly with his natural son, Arthur Jones. Ranelagh had been highly complimentary to Lillie in a lecherous kind of way when she was a visitor to his bungalow on the island. The noble lord, 64 years old, invited the couple to his lovely riverside home in Fulham for a picnic on the lawn. The Langtrys accepted

Lord Ranelagh. He made Lillie's career by introducing her into London society where she met the Prince of Wales.

with alacrity. Here Lillie met Lady Sebright who was much given to holding cultural Sunday soirées, attended by all manner of artists and politicians, at her house in Lavender Square. Lady Sebright shrewdly judged that Lillie would be more than welcome at such a gathering and duly invited her and her husband for the following Sunday. Lillie was not slow to accept.

It was a crowded affair. Lillie wore a simple black dress with a square-cut neckline, for she was still in mourning for her brother. She brushed her hair into a loose knot at the nape of her neck. She could not have been altogether unaware of how beautiful she looked, and she was indeed a sensation. In the course of that one evening she was practically mobbed by celebrities including the painters John Millais, James Whistler and Frank Miles and the celebrated actor

Henry Irving. Men fought to accompany her to dinner. Millais won. The Jersey Lily had arrived, stunningly beautiful, and fresh as a breath of clean air in the overheated, over-sexed, effete *fin-de-siècle* world of Victorian high society.

THE PRINCE OF WALES

Bertie, the Prince of Wales, over-indulged and under-employed, weak of chin and bandy-legged, more noted for his libido than his intellect, inevitably heard of this new, transcendentally beautiful addition to the London social scene. A meeting had to be arranged.

The prince's go-between was Captain Alan Young, adventurer and explorer. He had been much exercised of late to discover the Northwest Passage from the Atlantic through to the Pacific which would, if it existed at all, bind the huge British Empire even more closely together. He had not had much luck. In fact, he had discovered nothing at all but the endeavour was enough to gain him a knighthood. He was much admired in society. He was the man to lead the priapic prince panting to Lillie's side.

The prince's wife Alexandra, who grew mercifully deafer as the years went by, was away in Greece. Sir Alan arranged a discreet dinner party at his house early in 1877 to which he invited Lillie and her hapless, and increasingly alcoholic, husband. No one was let in on the secret that Bertie would attend. Lillie arrived and, if the gossips are right, she was breathtaking. Her complexion was as marvellously clear as ever, the eyes a piercing blue, the hair shining and casually fastened in the now-famous Langtry knot at the nape of the neck, the dress clinging tightly, provocatively to the uncorseted body. Was not she a dainty dish to set before a future king?

Indeed she was. Captain Young, or 'Alleno' as he was known to his intimates, seemed much distracted that night. He had no small talk and a curious faraway look in his eyes. He spoke but little. Lillie charitably put his strange manner down to his being an explorer; it is more likely that he was anxious for the meeting of the portly prince and the beautiful islander to go off without a hitch.

In her autobiography, Lillie described the prince's arrival: 'Suddenly there was a stir, followed by an expectant hush. A hurried exit of Sir Alan, then a slight commotion outside before presently I heard

The portly playboy, the Prince of Wales, as lecherous as he was vain. He wore his trousers creased at the sides to disguise his bandy legs.

a deep and cheery voice say, "I am afraid I am a little late." ' The prince entered. From duty to desire he had rushed, straight from a formal state function to Lillie's side. He was still gloriously festooned with glittering orders, medals and, most impressively, the blue ribbon of the Order of the Garter. Lillie was overcome and thought of climbing up the chimney to escape. She did not take this course of action but stayed, an excellent career move. The Prince of Wales was there for the taking. So was she. Lillie sank to the floor, offering him a deep curtsey as the gentle opening to the sensual dance. Charmingly decolletée, eyes wide, lips parted, she was wonderfully and excitingly available. Poor Mr Langtry at her side, surprised by the princely visitation, blushed and could hardly speak a word. Whether this was because of a sudden terrible realisation of what was happening in front of his very eyes, or a natural bashfulness before nobility, it was impossible to tell. Lillie took a perverse delight in observing his discomfiture. Perhaps she despised him; he was a social misfit whose usefulness to her was confined to his wallet.

Lillie paid obsequious and very careful attention to the words of the prince, venturing only modest murmurs of assent to his observations on the quality of the cooking, the promptness of the service and the bravery and courage of Sir Alan. That was all that was really necessary. His Highness was not so much interested in eloquence as availability, and when he left Alleno's house that night he must have had no doubt that he would see the luscious Lillie again. She, for her part, must have been in no doubt that she was about to reach the pinnacle of fame that could be achieved by a professional beauty. She had succeeded beyond her wildest, her most outrageous, dreams. She was to become the lover of the foremost prince in the British Empire.

In all conscience, their liaison cannot be described as a union of great minds. No marvellous literary correspondence sprang from their affair and, as far as can be told, there were no children. Beatrice and Dante they were not. Their relationship smacked, at least at first, more of naked opportunism than any deep love. He wanted sex with the most lovely professional beauty of the day and she wanted the glamour and the prestige and the luxury of being the prince's plaything, if only for a short time. Bertie was noted for nothing so much as the brevity of his liaisons. However, this was to be very unlike any of Bertie's previous affairs or, indeed, any of those which inevitably followed.

What their sexual relationship was like can only be guessed at. It is assumed by at least one of her biographers that Bertie, or 'His Nibs' as Lillie called him, must have been a peremptory and selfish lover, concerned only with his own enjoyment and not with that of the woman who was only there to serve him regardless of whether she felt pleasure or not. However, nobody can know of that intimate physical relationship. Lillie said absolutely nothing beyond that he did smell so of cigars – which would not necessarily prevent him from being an attentive and skilled lover. Indeed, it would be more surprising if he were not, having had so much practice with the outstanding courtesans of the day. It may be doubted, too, that Lillie simply lay back with Wales and thought of social advancement. She was after all a beautiful and sensual woman. No one can tell for certain. All is guesswork and conjecture, but whatever the species of intimacy in which they indulged, the fact of it directly and indirectly made Lillie's fortune and fame for the rest of her life.

Whereas Bertie had previously at least kept up the pretence of not having a mistress, he now positively flaunted the fact and Lillie revelled in the publicity and renown. She was introduced, on more than equal terms, to the aristocrats and gallants who formed the prince's Marlborough House set. She met the flower of English nobility. Many times Lillie appeared in public with the prince, seated next to him in his open carriage. They rode together along Rotten Row in the early mornings to the delight and astonishment of the gaping *hoi polloi*. Lillie felt like royalty, she had royalty, she was treated like royalty.

Her wardrobe increased dramatically in size commensurate with her new status. Gone was the plain black dress in which she had, seemingly effortlessly and artlessly, captured all hearts. In its place were extravagant creations from the best fashion designers. Gowns were flown in specially from Paris for every conceivable occasion and she ordered transparent negligés hemmed with sable to excite the predatory prince to even greater heights of sensual delight. To astonish and amaze the company at a Marlborough House ball she bought a dress made from yards of yellow tulle covered with gold netting, with 100 beautifully coloured butterflies caught up in the net.

Poor Edward Langtry. He had to foot the bill. He had to pay for the luxurious lifestyle of his fabulous wife, while the Prince of Wales comprehensively, publicly and carelessly cuckolded him. It is little wonder that he went into a decline, his fortune disappearing almost as fast as the drink in his glass. Not that Lillie cared too much for the poor fellow's discomfiture or his increasing absences on prolonged fishing trips. Her prince was building her a house. Other of his mistresses got baubles, rings or necklaces. Lillie got a beautiful house – the Red House at Bournemouth, which looked out over the wide Channel toward far-off Jersey. Along a wall in the dining-room was printed a legend redolent of her carefree island youth: 'They say – what say they? Let them say.'

It was the high summer of Lillie's society career. Everywhere she went she was mobbed; her dresses became the fashion of the time. Women wanted to look like her, dress like her, be like her. Lillie's

The Jersey Lily. At the height of her career she was the role model for every woman in society. Songs were written in her honour – or rather, because of her lack of it.

photograph was in all the shops, Lillie's name on everyone's lips.

One person who very much desired to see Lillie was the morose, melancholic Queen Victoria herself. She, with some reason, regarded Bertie as something of a fool and a great liability. She must have been aware of her son's affair with the Jersey Lily and, animated perhaps by the fear of scandal or by plain old-fashioned curiosity, decided to have a closer look at the woman. Lillie was to be presented to the queen. If nothing else, this would give her a degree of respectability and a place in society she would not otherwise have enjoyed. She must have been delighted at such a signal honour. But she must also have been a little nervous. The queen might, by a look or single remark in public, destroy her for good and all. Lillie decided to play the game to its utmost.

Her outfit was, to put it mildly, extravagant. It was also, and unexpectedly, very witty. She was dressed by her aunt and her mother in a low-cut dress of ivory brocade, dotted with artificial yellow Maréchal Niel roses that matched the bouquet Bertie had thoughtfully and lovingly sent to her that very morning. The court train was all of 9 feet long and hung from her shoulders after the fashion of Napoleon's Josephine. The queen had declared a dislike of the small, nay tiny, feathers with which society ladies had taken to adorning their gowns and hair. The Lord Chamberlain conveyed this information to all interested parties, insisting that the feathers were at least to be visible to the naked eye. Lillie's feather adornment was certainly that. She acquired three of the largest ostrich plumes available and wore them on her head. There was certainly no danger of the myopic sovereign missing those.

There was, however, more to the wearing of the feathers than consideration for the queen's eyesight. The three swaying feathers were more than reminiscent of the Prince of Wales' coat of arms, which also featured three plumes. Observers might also have been reminded of the motto which went with the prince's feathers: 'I serve'. Perhaps, however, such an outrageous outfit was never intended for the queen's sight. Lillie was a long way down the list of those to be presented and she knew that Victoria, easily fatigued by such occasions, would in all probability have left before it was her turn to be presented. The Princess of Wales, accompanied by Bertie, would then take over and receive Mrs Langtry. If Lillie believed this would happen her behaviour was, if anything, even more outrageous: she, the mistress of the prince, would be presenting herself unabashedly

Lillie was acknowledged as an outstanding beauty of an original kind. Most of our images of her come from rather stiff, unnatural photographs and it is difficult for us to understand the love and admiration she excited. Occasionally, however, we catch some small glimpse of her sensual beauty.

on a public state occasion to his wife, the Princess of Wales.

In the event, the black and shrouded queen found the stamina, or possibly the curiosity, to stay until everyone had been presented, including Lillie. If she saw the humour of Lillie's attire she was not amused one little bit. There were many such occasions in her life. In Lillie's words, the queen 'looked straight in front of her and I thought extended out her hand in a rather perfunctory manner. There was not even a flicker of a smile on her face, and she looked grave and tired.' After the nerve-racking ceremony, Lillie reflected that, 'After hours of waiting in the crush room of the palace, penned like sheep, with a heavy train folded on the arm and constant dragging of the white tulle veil, to be seen only for a moment as each of us hurried in and out of the presence, made it seem a great deal of labour lost.' And perhaps the waving ostrich feathers had been just a little too much. She consoled herself that May night by going to a ball with Bertie at Marlborough House.

Bertie went everywhere with Lillie. He would not attend society dinners or visit his aristocratic friends unless she was invited too. She accompanied him to Cowes and stayed aboard *Osborne*, the royal yacht, for days of passion and merry japes in the company of the idle rich. Lillie loved the life and delighted, with the rest of the Marlborough House set, in carefree juvenile larks such as piercing holes in hot-water bottles or sliding down stairs on silver trays to win a bet.

But Edward Langtry's money was running out and he had to sell the Southampton house and his yacht. His creditors were pressing. Then there was the Press. Admittedly it was much less intrusive, and certainly more circumspect, than the Press of today. But it could still create a great deal of pain and trouble for someone who was thought to have strayed even a little from the straight and narrow, particularly if that someone was the heir to the throne.

In the autumn of 1879, Adolphus Rosenburg, the proprietor of *Town Talk* magazine, increased its circulation dramatically by reporting that no less a person than His Royal Highness the Prince of Wales, together with those illustrious peers of the realm Lord Lonsborough and Lord Lonsdale, was to be cited by Mr Edward Langtry in an action against his wife for divorce. There was no direct and immediate response from the parties concerned but a careful listener would have heard everywhere the distinct, if discreet, shuffle of feet as the Establishment closed ranks.

On 8 October 1879, Rosenburg published the startling news that Mr Edward Langtry had dropped his intended action against Mrs Langtry, and that he would probably be departing for some important diplomatic post abroad. The statement was not at all beyond the bounds of probability but, unfortunately, not at all easy to substantiate. It was time for the kill. On 25 October, 27-year-old Adolphus Rosenburg of Brixton was brought to the Old Bailey, before an unforgiving Mr Justice Hawkins, and charged with criminal libel.

Edward Langtry had miraculously acquired the services of very expensive counsel in the shape of Sergeant Parry. Asked if there was any truth in the stories of his wife's infidelities published in *Town Talk*, Edward, remarkably sober, replied that there was not. He had always lived on terms of affection with his wife and, indeed, was doing so now. In other words, they were a blameless couple leading virtuous lives together in their house at Norfolk Street and, in an ideal world free of liars like Rosenburg, no taint of scandal should ever have attached to them. He was also asked if he had been offered any kind of diplomatic post abroad. He replied no. The wretched Rosenburg was found guilty as charged and sentenced to 18 months imprisonment, the judge characteristically expressing great regret that he could not add hard labour. The sensitive Lillie was spared the trauma of giving evidence in this sorry trial. She and Bertie had gone to Paris together and afterwards to Cowes. There she met Prince Louis of Battenberg, serving as a lieutenant aboard the royal yacht.

Battenberg was a devilish handsome fellow, nephew to the Prince of Wales, with whom he compared more than favourably in terms of physical attraction. He was younger, taller, fitter and much more handsome with blue eyes, dark hair and a fine manly beard. Beyond question he was an aristocrat and, for some little time, he enjoyed life as one of the prince's set. He spent weekends up at Marlborough House, where he inevitably met Lillie, as he did when Bertie and she came down to Cowes. Louis and Lillie became lovers. Prince Edward seemed not to mind. True to his character, he himself had been unfaithful to Lillie at least once with the latest beauty, Sarah Bernhardt, imported into the market from France courtesy of the Comédie-Française. Perhaps he liked the idea of his young, handsome nephew enjoying what he had enjoyed. Or perhaps they simply shared her for a time. Nobody knows.

What is known is that Lillie was dining at Marlborough House with the prince and the saintlike Princess Alexandra when she experienced a sudden sharp pain in her stomach. She had to excuse herself and return home to lie down. The Princess Alexandra was so concerned for Lillie's health that she sent her own physician, Francis Laking, to attend to her. The next afternoon, Alexandra called in person. Lillie tried to rise from her *chaise-longue* to greet the princess, but Alexandra would have none of that and told her to stay where she was while she poured the tea. They chatted in desultory fashion about the violet perfume Alexandra was wearing and similar trivia, but the princess must have known from Laking that Lillie had become pregnant.

The question was, and is: which of the two men in Lillie's life at that time was the father? The Prince of Wales was widely thought to be responsible and took very little trouble to deny it. He may have believed that being thought to have fathered Lillie's child merely enhanced his reputation as a dashing Lothario. More interestingly, he might have let people assume he was the father because he had a shrewd suspicion that Louis Battenberg's career would be ruined if he, rather than the prince, was named as the father. Perhaps none of the three people involved – Lillie, Bertie and Louis – knew for certain who had fathered little Jeanne-Marie although, in later life, Lillie always swore it was Battenberg.

Times were getting difficult for Lillie. She was pregnant and professional beauties were not supposed to get pregnant. Moreover, she was increasingly worried by debt. Edward Langtry's revenues from Ireland were drying up completely. There was no more money forthcoming to finance Lillie's extraordinary lifestyle. The bailiffs came knocking on the door at Norfolk Street. Lillie tells how her ever-faithful Italian maid, Dominique, 'never missed an opportunity of cramming my few trinkets and other treasured trifles and indeed anything portable into the pockets of anyone who came to visit me. In this way some very distinguished friends departed from the beleaguered house with their pockets full, all unconscious they were evading the law.' It is rumoured that Bertie himself assisted in this illegal removal of goods by secreting a little gold-backed mirror in his inside pocket when he left after a visit. He might have thought it a joke, but for Lillie it was the turning-point in her career. She was bankrupt and pregnant. Her career as the foremost professional beauty in English society was slipping away from her; soon it would be gone for ever.

One night, at the Duchess of Westminster's ball at Grosvenor

Louis Battenberg, the handsome fellow who Lillie swore was the father of her daughter. Lillie did not tell Jeanne-Marie who her father was until many years after her birth. When she did, it caused a terrible rift with her daughter.

House, the realisation hit home. Most of the people she knew had great responsibility in the land or were artists or workers of some kind. She, in wretched contrast, was utterly idle with no more than a decorative role to play in the great drama of life. 'My anomalous position once realised, I began to lose interest in my daily round of amusement, until it became unendurable.' Thus Lillie rather poetically described her state. In more prosaic terms, she knew that, as far as her career as a professional beauty and mistress to royalty was concerned, the end was in sight. It was not elevated spiritual insight into her condition that made her change her ways, but a hard-headed assessment of the options that were available.

She consulted her friends. Frank Miles volunteered the ludicrous advice that she should take up market gardening. Oscar Wilde was understandably less than enthusiastic about this, saying that Frank would, 'Compel the Lillie to tramp the fields in muddy boots.' Such a career was unthinkable. Whistler believed Lillie should become an artist like himself; yet others urged her to take up millinery or dressmaking. Irving suggested she become an actress.

Lillie delayed making any decision, but she knew her life would have to change, and radically. She returned to Jersey in 1880 to keep her pregnancy secret. Edward Langtry never knew of her state at this time, although Lillie was very fearful he might find out. Bertie had sent him to Chicago, and then to New York, on some fool's errand which kept him out of the country for the required period. Lillie had time to think. She turned to an old friend, Arthur Jones, Lord Ranelagh's natural son, who lived in Jersey.

Love letters written between 1878 and 1882 have been discovered couched in the most affectionate of terms. It seems certain that they had a passionate relationship at some time. The details are scarce, but it was to Arthur she turned for help and comfort at this most trying period of her life. Lillie could not have the child in Jersey, nor indeed England, for fear of a great scandal implicating the royal family. She would have to go to France, where delicate matters of parentage could more easily be concealed. In the deep, icy winter of that year Lillie set sail for France in a small boat.

She may have reflected bitterly how far she had come from the bright lights and adulation of the Marlborough House set. How far from lying in the arms of the heir apparent, basking in his patronage, breathing in the rich cigar smoke. How far, indeed, from any comfort she had travelled in the short space of 6 months.

Arthur Jones, Jersey farmer and clubman, to whom Lillie wrote passionate love-letters. The natural son of the old roué Lord Ranelagh, his liaison with Lillie has only recently been discovered.

On the Monday after a seemingly endless journey to Paris, Lillie was deeply depressed and wrote a passionate letter to her Jersey lover, 'My darling Arthur' as she called him. She begged him to let his island farm as he had promised and rush to her side because she missed him so and was so miserable, and loved him so much. Lillie also sent him a telegram which read simply: 'Do come, not ill but so miserable.' She was being looked after at this time by a Dr Pratt who was answerable to Mr Clayton, a creature of Prince Edward. He, in turn, had orders to ensure that Lillie was kept as deep in hiding as possible while she had her baby even if, as Lillie caustically remarked, it meant living in the middle of a wood. The Establishment was being very careful indeed.

It is extraordinary to reflect that at the time of her sojourn in France she was having Louis Battenberg's baby, she had a continuing relationship with the Prince of Wales, she was married to Edward Langtry and, at the same time, passionately and deeply in love with Arthur Jones. Her emotional life was nothing if not rich.

A later letter to Arthur, or 'Artie', told how she had finally found an apartment in the Champs-Elysées, very reasonably priced, she thought, at 1100 francs a month. In the meantime, however, Lillie had received a nasty shock. Edward Langtry who, as Lillie said, drove her mad with his absolute refusal to give her a divorce, had been in touch saying he was going to write to her concerning an important matter. This frightened her inordinately, for she now supposed he knew about her pregnancy and her travels to Paris. Worm she might consider him to be, but he could turn. Perhaps he would drag her and the Prince of Wales and Louis Battenberg back with him to the Old Bailey Court, but this time with a different story to tell.

Lillie need not have worried. Edward Langtry knew nothing of his wife's pregnancy and was merely concerned about what he was supposed to be doing in America where no one had heard of him or his errand. It was not until many years later that he learned what had happened and by then he was destitute and too ill to care.

Little Jeanne-Marie Langtry was born into the world early in 1881. For the first 14 years of her life she was led to believe that Lillie was her aunt. When she discovered that she was in fact her mother, she was not disabused of the notion that Edward Langtry was her father. Jeanne-Marie continued in this belief until she was twenty-one and about to be married to a member of the Scottish aristocracy, Ian Malcolm of the Clan MacCallum. When she found out the truth, the consequences were devastating indeed.

A THEATRICAL CAREER

Lillie knew that she had to fend for herself and her child. She had few qualifications for any sort of real work. All she had was her beauty, her notoriety and, as it turned out, a remarkable and indomitable ambition to be financially secure. She remembered Irving's advice and Oscar Wilde's opinion that she should take up a career on the stage. At 28 years old, this is what she did. During the course of three decades she performed in theatres the length and breadth of Britain, all across the United States of America and even in South Africa. Despite all this practice, however, she never became a truly great actress, a second Sarah Bernhardt or another Ellen Terry. She advanced slowly but steadily from mediocrity to competence, but not much further. One critic, comparing Lillie Langtry to Helena Modjeska, a popular actress of European extraction, wrote, 'The difference between Modjeska and Lillie Langtry is that the first is a Pole and the other a stick.' But audiences didn't jam theatres across the world to see her act. They came not as lovers of the drama but rather as voyeurs to see in the flesh that sensual woman who had been the prince's plaything. The theatre became a zoo and she a major exhibit. If she cared about this, she never said.

Henrietta Labouchère it was, wife of the radical Member of Parliament Henry Labouchère, who encouraged Lillie to take her first, and understandably faltering, steps on to the stage and undertook to show her the rudiments of acting. Lillie remarks in her autobiography, 'I should like to put her name in capitals of gratitude for she determined my future through her sheer pertinacity and launched me on a career of pleasurable striving after the unattainable.'

Lillie's first major part was in 1881 as Kate Hardcastle in Oliver Goldsmith's *She Stoops to Conquer*, at a matinée for the benefit of the theatrical fund at the Haymarket Theatre. Some of the most celebrated actors on the London stage were to complete the cast. Lillie described how, on the day of the performance, 'Crowds waited for many hours outside the pit and gallery doors for the opening time, buoyed up with sandwiches and other refreshments, while those blessed with extra foresight had come provided also with camp stools.' The theatre was packed as never before. Many of Lillie's friends, and a lot of her enemies, were there. Lords and ladies jostled to get the better seats. The Duchess of Manchester was there with a large party and, most important, the Prince and Princess of Wales arrived to witness the debut, she looking a little melancholic but he chubby and cheerful as a pigeon. The curtain finally went up and the play began. Lillie made her entrance.

There were a few titters, even a hiss or two from the gallery, but Mrs Labouchère had done her work well and Lillie appeared totally unperturbed by these noises, although she confessed later that she

Lillie as Kate Hardcastle in *She Stoops to Conquer*. It was her first appearance on the professional stage.

had been more than a little disconcerted by seeing quite clearly all the faces in the auditorium.

In truth, all she had to do was stand up, not knock the furniture over and be beautiful. She managed all these things with considerable aplomb and this was more than enough to ensure her success. Lillie took many curtain calls and received a generally favourable press, *The Times* advocating that Mrs Langtry's next role should undoubtedly be Lady Teazle in Sheridan's great comedy *The School for Scandal*. There were, it is true to say, a few bad notices. A critic from *Punch* remarked that Lillie's 'action is as constrained and mechanical as that of an Eton sixth form boy on speech day'. In the stage journal *Era*, the critic opined that Mrs Langtry was at most 'a respectable amateur'. Lillie was to receive scores of such reviews and worse, much worse, in the years to come, but they scarcely affected the box-office.

She left the Haymarket and went on a grand tour of the provinces. Everywhere she went, people flocked into the streets, to the railway stations and into the theatres to see the fabulous Jersey Lily. Everywhere, every ticket was sold. After one performance at the Prince's Theatre in Manchester, young gallants gathered round her carriage and, after applauding and hurrahing her to the very echo, unhitched the horses and dragged the coach back to her hotel. The experience was repeated in Glasgow. Students in Belfast presented her with a flock of fluttering doves tied with blue ribbons to a floral cage. Lillie was everywhere triumphant.

She returned to London and achieved even greater acclaim, if that were possible, playing Rosalind in *As You Like It*. Not for her acting it has to be said, but for her legs, sensationally revealed by doublet and hose to anyone who could afford a ticket. The punters could enjoy, from the comfort of their seats, some of the physical attributes that had aroused so much royal blood. They were apparently still arousing it; the Prince of Wales, in a fit of rare enthusiasm, came to both the gala night and the opening night. It was indeed the prince who encouraged Lillie to turn her thoughts towards America. Lillie and Henrietta thought it an excellent idea. After all, Sarah Bernhardt had made fabulous amounts of money in New York the year before, so why shouldn't Lillie follow in her footsteps? It is true she could not act anywhere near as well as the amazing Bernhardt, but she had been to bed with the same prince of the realm. If Lillie's experience in London was anything to go by, that would be more than enough to guarantee a similar success.

AMERICA AND THE MONEY MEN

Henry E. Abbey, swarthy and fat, who had been responsible for introducing Sarah Bernhardt to America, came post-haste to arrange a similar trip for the famous Jersey courtesan. Lillie proved to be a hard-headed businesswoman but a deal was eventually struck. She was to get the same money as Sarah Bernhardt: 50 per cent of all the box-office above $4000, $1000 per performance and all hotel expenses. Further, all the costs to Lillie's company – hotel bills, salaries and wardrobe maintenance – were to be met by Abbey himself. He went back to New York and began a tremendous publicity campaign to promote Lillie's visit, always and ever pointing up the fact that it was the prince's mistress who was about to appear before the public's wonder-wounded eyes.

In October 1882, Lillie and Henrietta Labouchère embarked from Liverpool on the fast but rat-infested steamship *Arizona*. The rats were long-coated and disconcertingly tame. Henrietta awoke one night to find a fat and very friendly rodent nestling on her chest. The crossing was without incident and after 16 days at sea the little *Arizona* chugged into port at New York. Henry Abbey and his partner Schoeffel had prepared well for Lillie's arrival. A tug, boasting a brass band and packed from stem to stern with reporters, pulled alongside. There, unmistakably, was the exotic Oscar Wilde, extravagant as ever, waving a bunch of lilies at her.

It was a wonderful beginning to her American experience. Lillie elected to wear a simple black dress around the city, the same design that had caused such a sensation when she was first introduced into London society. It had been a good trick then and it was a good trick now. Everywhere she went, there were reporters with endless questions. She replied to them with great diplomacy, expressing great enthusiasm for all things American. Everywhere she went, she was instantly recognised and lavishly fêted. Lillie was a sensation. The theatre seats for the opening night were put up for auction. They were all sold. The auction raised $20 000.

The best publicity, however, was provided unintentionally, or so it is thought. Lillie was resting, reclining on her *chaise-longue* in her hotel room, at about 5 o'clock on the afternoon of the day before the opening. Suddenly, a friend from England, Pierre Lavaloud, burst into the room shouting that the theatre was on fire. Indeed it was. Lillie could see it from her bedroom window. The conflagration had started in the carpentry rooms and spread quickly and unchecked to engulf the entire building. Broadway was crammed with spectators of this unexpected and free show. The flames burst through the theatre roof as Lillie watched intently. Only the wooden sign with her name emblazoned upon it, high above the theatre on an iron scaffold, seemed to escape the flames. Lillie watched. 'If it stands, I shall succeed,' she said, adding quickly as the flames mounted ever higher and as the sign seemed to be tumbling, 'If it burns, I will succeed without it.' It stood.

Abbey quickly transferred the show to another theatre and, with a great deal of work and improvisation, it opened just 1 week later.

The play with which Lillie launched her campaign to win America was called *An Unequal Match*. It was a very tedious drama, as she freely admitted, in which she played Hester Grazebrook, an illiterate milkmaid, who is seduced by a baronet who then marries her. A whole act, no less, was devoted to Hester philosophising in rustic manner on the nature of her new position. Her peasant naivety drives her husband, Sir Harry, into the arms of a beautiful, scheming seductress. In the last act Hester is transformed miraculously into a sophisticated lady of the world and, employing her new-found skills, sees off the hussy and wins back her husband. Not the stuff guaranteed to widen the eyes and make the pulses race – in fact, the very reverse, as the critics were not slow to point out.

Matters didn't improve when Lillie appeared in the company's second offering: *As You Like It* by the great William Shakespeare. Even the old trick of appearing in tights, to show off the legs that had been caressed by a prince, failed to dissipate the ennui which descended like a fog over the audience, many of whom left halfway through. The New York season could not be described as an unalloyed triumph. Much more interesting than Lillie's on-stage performances were her off-stage exploits.

Freddie Gebhard was the first of an increasingly bizarre series of men with whom Lillie had affairs. It did not seem to matter that they were shallow and trivial, and had never properly matured. It did not seem to matter that they were drunken, dissolute or vicious. What did matter was that they all had a great deal of money and were willing to pay Lillie handsomely for the pleasures with which she provided them. Freddie was an over-indulged juvenile. The barely literate 22-year-old son of a Baltimore dry goods businessman, he had inherited somewhere in the region of $6 million and a substantial annual income on his father's death. He was tall, youthfully slim and beautifully dressed in the best that money could buy. He liked to drink a lot, he liked the ladies a lot and he liked to gamble a lot. This dark-haired, handsome 'boudoir carriage Romeo', as he came to be known, counted among his talents an ability to render a perfect imitation of a cock crowing. Very apt. He was not a serious man. He was vainglorious and ignorant and destined to die young at forty-six, but he was besotted with Lillie and bought his way into her affection and her bed.

He besieged her hotel room; he showered her with expensive gifts; he gave her blank cheques to buy whatever she wanted at Tiffanys, the best jewellers in the world. She, enamoured of such wealth, conducted the affair with vigour and at the expense of rehearsals for *As You Like It*. Henrietta Labouchère, outraged by her pupil's lack of professional application, and even more outraged by Lillie selling herself to the highest bidder, departed the scene for Washington. Undeterred, Lillie took over the running of the company herself and embarked on a coast-to-coast tour of America. She took Freddie along for the ride and the publicity.

The critics were almost uniformly hostile, but it did not matter. The scandalously wicked affair of Gebhard and Langtry made headlines wherever they went. The theatres were consequently packed. Freddie was, indeed, very good for publicity and almost as famous as Lillie herself. His behaviour ensured that she featured in many a newspaper headline. He attacked and knocked down a man he judged to be bothering his mistress, and challenged a reporter from the *Globe* to a duel for denouncing himself and Lillie as gross sinners. Freddie was very good for business.

Lillie was denounced in the House of Representatives, as Sarah Bernhardt had been before her, as a harlot who should be sent back to England forthwith. It was all wonderful for the box-office. She did have a few qualms about the more lurid tirades directed at her. She invited her husband Edward's sister, the very proper Agnes Langtry, across the Atlantic to be her chaperone in the rather forlorn hope that this would give some virtue to her character. It was a ludicrous ploy, doomed to failure. The upright Agnes found Freddie and Lillie half-naked in bed together one night at a hotel. Shocked, she left for England the next morning.

Gebhard wanted desperately to marry Lillie. There was nothing he would not do, nothing he would not buy, to please her. At the end of the American tour, which earned Lillie a massive profit of $100 000, she departed for England to try and persuade Edward Langtry to give her a divorce. The wretched fellow must have read the reports in all the newspapers but he was nevertheless immovable. Publicly humiliated, cuckolded time without number, he would allow no divorce. Disappointed, she returned to New York.

Freddie had bought a splendid house for her: 362 West 23rd Street. It was surrounded by exotic gardens and fitted with marble baths and designs of polished walnut. More than this, however, he bought Lillie her very own private railway car at a staggering cost of $250 000. It was 70 feet long, made from polished teak and painted blue. It had ten rooms including a fully equipped kitchen, a maid's room and two guest rooms. The centrepiece of this mobile palace was Lillie's bedroom which was the last word in luxury, upholstered in padded silk brocade. The bathroom had solid silver fittings. The living-room was furnished with green and cream brocade from France. Lillie christened it 'The Lalee'.

In this extraordinary vehicle she toured America. Never one for understatement, she behaved as if she were royalty. It was not so much a theatrical tour as a royal progress. Everywhere there was an audience – and there was an audience everywhere – Lillie would perform. She played where no theatre company had ever played before. She played all across the American Midwest. She played the glittering and sophisticated theatres of San Francisco and the tin sheds of New Mexico with equal aplomb. Simple cowpokes, squatting on their haunches, haughty socialites in Paris finery, would-be lovers and would-be detractors, all came to see the phenomenon of the age – slightly plumper than of yore, it is true, but none the less the apotheosis of allure and forbidden sensuality. Judge Roy Bean, the 'Law West of Pecos', who ruled Vinagroon in south Texas, renamed the town Langtry after her. Between her tours of America, Lillie (and Freddie) returned to Britain.

America gave Lillie the opportunity to be rid of Edward Langtry for good. The Californian divorce laws were significantly laxer than those in England and she pressed them to her service. Poor Edward was outflanked. In 1897, she gained her divorce, and custody of Jeanne-Marie, after a very private meeting in a Judge Crump's chambers in Lakestown, California. The grounds for the divorce were that she had long since been deserted by her husband! Lillie was now free to marry Freddie Gebhard.

Lillie's signature on a card now in the Jersey Museum. Her writing was large and extrovert: she could make one short sentence take up a whole page.

She did not do so. She now lived openly with him in America, but she would not marry him. Perhaps she had never really intended to, even though he had bought her all that money could buy, including a huge ranch of 7500 acres in California. He stocked this, at vast expense, with thoroughbred horses, gun dogs, sheep, exotic chickens, ducks, geese and ornamental fish. He laid out a railway track all around the sprawling property so that The Lalee could traverse the estate. It was all to no avail. Lillie hardly bothered to visit the ranch. Their relationship went into an irreversible decline. More and more, Freddie realised the extent to which Lillie was using him simply and brazenly to provide money. He was also jealous of the Prince of Wales' renewed interest in her. It is rumoured that the final break came when Freddie burst into Lillie's bedroom to find her and Bertie locked in an amorous embrace. Moreover, his fortune had been decimated by the high-spending Lillie and he suffered more financial strain when he lost nearly $500 000 worth of bloodstock in a train crash in Pennsylvania.

Used by Lillie much as Edward Langtry had been used, Freddie saw less and less of a future with her. They quarrelled bitterly and he left. Very soon afterwards he married the lovely Louise Morris, a Baltimore heiress. Her money went some way to restore his ailing fortunes but the marriage did not last. In 1910, he died of alcoholism, much as Edward had done some years before, at the age of forty-six. Another extravagant lover of Lillie's was to die of drink.

THE SQUIRE

George Alexander Baird, or 'Squire Abington' as he was known, was a lout. A young man for whom the term 'yahoo' might have been specially invented. He was the only child of George and Cecilia Baird of Edinburgh. His father was fabulously wealthy, his fortune derived from the Scottish iron and coal industry. He died in 1876, leaving George, then 15 years old, in the tender, loving care of a foolish mother who indulged her son in every possible way. He had scarcely any formal education. Although his mother sent him to Eton he refused to stay there very long. He remarked that he didn't much care for the place and left. He later went to Cambridge but it is doubtful if he learned anything there beyond how to ride a horse.

Semi-literate and immature, he thrust himself into society where he soon made a reputation – and not a good reputation – for himself. He was surrounded with all kinds of spongers, hangers-on and ne'er-do-wells. He pursued a life of excess with never a moment's respite. He loved cockfighting, dogfighting, whoring, boxing and, above all else, drinking.

He was good at one thing and one thing only: riding horses. At this he was brilliant. As an amateur rider he took on, and defeated, some of the best professionals of the day, although he was banned for 2 years by the Jockey Club for 'foul' riding. He returned from this exile and continued to enjoy enormous success all through the 1880s. He was of average height, with a large head and a prominent jaw, and very thin indeed. He would deliberately starve himself to get down to his racing weight of below 10 stones. This endless process of purging, or wasting, coupled with his degenerate lifestyle inevitably brought about his early death. It was this amoral creature, loathed, feared and ostracised by all respectable society, who took the Jersey Lily for his mistress. It was as unlikely an alliance as one could wish for and could be explained by one, and only one, factor: his money. Lillie would suffer a lot for that.

Their first meeting took place by chance at Newmarket Races on 28 April 1891. Lillie had loved horses ever since those far-off days in Jersey when, full of the joys of youth, she had galloped her horse along the sands of St Aubin's Bay and captured the heart of at least one young man. George told her to back his horse Quartus, and encouraged her further by promising to give her three times the amount of her original stake if the beast lost. Eventually, she took his advice and backed his horse and another that the Squire recommended. Both horses romped home in fine style and the Squire romped his way into Lillie's bed. Society laughed at the incongruity of the liaison, but let them laugh; Lillie had found another wallet to plunder.

She herself, however, suffered grievously for her greed. Along with his other charming traits, George quickly showed that he had an ungovernable, vicious temper. When he was not fondling her shamelessly in public, he was beating her up in private. Lillie's friends were amazed, and made the not unreasonable enquiry as to why she endured such behaviour. Lillie replied, revealingly, that though she hated him he gave her a cheque for £5000 every time he beat her.

On one occasion, while George was in Scotland, Lillie in search of gentler pleasures went with Robert Peel to Paris. Robert, grandson of the famous Peel who, as home secretary, established the first disciplined police force in London, was amiable and rich but, more important, he was gentle with her. It must have been a welcome relief. However, any joy was short-lived. George, incensed that his famous mistress should go off with someone else, followed them hotfoot to France and, discovering them in their hotel bedroom, knocked Robert to the floor. In his drunken fit he beat Lillie herself into a bleeding heap, then tore off her clothes and raped her. As a result of his attentions Lillie was in hospital for 2 weeks. She issued a warrant for his arrest but suddenly dropped all proceedings against him. The reasons were not far to seek. Contrite, George offered Lillie a cheque for £50 000 and the outright gift of a 222-foot yacht, the *Whyte Lady*, if she would forgive him. Lillie forgave him and accepted the gifts with equal alacrity. It was a highly profitable affair for Lillie, but it was undoubtedly the spiritual nadir of her career.

George Baird's drunken progress through the world came to a mercifully abrupt end on 18 March 1893 in New Orleans. The Squire had gone there to watch the champion boxer, Bob Fitzsimmons, fight Jem Hall. There was an extraordinary drinking bout during and after the fight. George fell ill with pneumonia. He was only 38 years old, but his constitution was so undermined by debauchery and dissipation that he could offer no resistance whatsoever and died.

Lillie was cruising in the Mediterranean aboard the *Whyte Lady*, unkindly nicknamed the *Black Eye*, when she heard the news of George Baird's death. She must have thought she was in luck. She believed that the Squire would remember her in his will and, with unseemly haste, landed at Nice and raced to Paris then to London to discover George's final wishes. It was a wasted journey. Not a penny of his huge £8 million fortune had been left to her. All the money was to be distributed among members of his family. No one who was unrelated to him by blood was included.

Lillie went back to the rest of her life. George had given her a colt called Milford and, under the name Mr Jersey, she started her own string of highly successful racehorses. She bought a house, Regal Lodge, at Newmarket to be close to the racing fraternity. The house was aptly named. The Prince of Wales followed her to Newmarket shortly afterwards, residing at Eggerton House. He became a more than an occasional visitor at Lillie's 'cottage', as she described Regal Lodge – although it had twenty servants, seven bedrooms and an ornamental fishpond, with goldfish, in the drawing-room. The prince's continuing affection for Lillie undoubtedly helped rehabilitate her in so-called respectable society after the appalling and unappetising affair with Baird. Life was almost back to normal.

Secure in the prince's affection, Lillie continued her stage career. She toured the United States in 1894 and was again hugely successful. The plays she appeared in, such as *A Wife's Peril* and *Gossip*, were rubbishy melodramas and she herself was little more than a clothes horse, but everywhere people fought to see her. The same was true when she played in London. The second half of the nineties seems to have been the most happy and contented time of her life. She enjoyed social gatherings, she still had the love of a prince, her reputation on stage was miraculously undimmed and, above all, she was financially secure and self-sufficient. Lillie could enjoy life, and even enjoy stories against herself such as the scurrilous joke in a scandal rag called *The Pinkun*: 'We heard Mrs Langtry has lost her parrot; for this we are sorry. That the lady possessed such a bird, we were unaware but we knew she had a cockatoo.' It was as well she had been brought up with six brothers.

It was at this time of Lillie's renaissance in society that the unfortunate, pathetic and deluded Edward Langtry died horribly and painfully in Cheshire County Lunatic Asylum on 15 October 1897. Bitter and depressed at the treatment meted out to him by his wife, and especially ashamed by the divorce, Edward had become a confirmed alcoholic. He was discovered staggering about Crewe station, dishevelled, with injuries to his face and head. He was taken to a police station and his wounds were dressed. Edward then left the station and headed for the nearest public house. He was·later found, unconscious and stinking of alcohol, in a cab yard. He regained consciousness but began babbling incoherently, and was sent to the county lunatic asylum in Chester. He survived only a few hours. The verdict at the inquest into how this unhappiest of men died was accidental death.

Lillie sent a wreath to his funeral done out in her racing colours, which some observers considered to be an exquisitely cruel and offensive gesture: her horse Merman had just won the Cesarewitch.

LADY DE BATHE

Lillie had a new little house back home in Jersey and she named it after her greatest winner. It was Merman Cottage, on the south coast of the island, and a close friend she had met at Newmarket came to visit her there. Hugo de Bathe was good looking, boyishly handsome and weak-willed. He was 20 years younger than Lillie and had very little money. However, none of this mattered very much for he would have something to give her which she had ever wanted, but could never buy: a title.

Hugo's father, Sir Hugo de Bathe, was old and when he died his son would inherit the title and his not inconsiderable fortune. If Lillie married young Hugo she would become Lady de Bathe. This was a prize indeed and in 1899 the couple were duly married in an empty St Saviour's church, high above St Helier, where her libidinous father, the 'dirty dean', had preached for many a long year. Not unnaturally, Hugo's father objected to the union of his son to such a conspicuous courtesan and cut him out of his will. Fortunately, old Sir Henry forgave Hugo after the young man had fought in the South African Wars (1899–1902).

When Sir Henry died in 1905, Lillie duly became Lady de Bathe. She never bothered to see very much at all of her husband, even after his return from the war. She was to see even less of her daughter, the now grown up and desirable Jeanne-Marie.

Jeanne-Marie was 21 years old in 1902, and was about to be married to Ian Malcolm, a Scottish aristocrat. Margot Asquith, ever a trouble-maker and gossip, told her something she had never known, or even suspected: her father was Louis of Battenberg. Not Uncle

Overleaf: L'Ile au Guerlain, Le Portelet. This shows the house where Arthur Jones lived, to which Lillie was a frequent visitor.

Below: Lillie as Lady de Bathe. She was 20 years older than her titled husband and the couple saw little of each other.

Maurice as she was first told – he was one of Lillie's brothers, and Jeanne-Marie had believed Lillie was her aunt – nor Edward Langtry as she was later informed, not even the new King Edward as she had heard rumoured, but Louis Battenberg. The naturally distraught girl confronted her mother with the fact and Lillie confirmed it. But she was not content just to do that. She went further and callously told her daughter that it was better her father was someone like Louis than a drunken sot like Edward Langtry. That was the end of the relationship. After the wedding, Jeanne-Marie refused to have anything more to do with her mother. Lillie was distraught and wrote heartfelt and pleading letters to Jeanne, begging to see her. Her daughter's reply was emphatic: 'I suffered the last day under your roof knowing this change to have come upon me, yet powerless to alter it. In future we had best live our own lives apart. In conclusion, please believe me that painful though I know it must be for you to receive this letter, the necessity of writing it causes the most intense misery to your daughter. Jeanne.'

It was a body blow, but Lillie does not mention it in her autobiography. Her life continued much as usual. She toured America in appalling plays, one of which she wrote herself. She went on tour in South Africa and toured the provinces in Britain in plays like *The Degenerates*, which had caused riots across America although it was quite well received when she played it at the little Opera House in Jersey. The plot of the play mirrored almost exactly the scandalous events of Lillie's own dalliance with the Prince of Wales. Much self-righteous criticism was directed at such behaviour being portrayed on a public stage. Lillie must have enjoyed the paradoxical situation. Her best acting, however, had been reserved for playing the role of the hero's wife.

After Hugo de Bathe's departure to fight in South Africa shortly after their wedding, Lillie had given histrionic displays to anyone who would listen of how much she loved and missed him. She even kept a map of the South African theatre of operations in her dressing-room, with flags to mark the whereabouts of the young Hugo. She was playing in Chicago when she received news that Hugo had been injured. She collapsed weeping at each interval – although she bravely managed to continue the performance to the end. This touching behaviour was well-publicised.

Despite her very public protestations of affection for her husband, Lillie still found time to take another lover: Edward Cohen. He was to be her last. Like most of the others, he had prodigious quantities of money, gained from his racehorses. He was a friend of King Edward, and not at all averse to sampling the same pleasures that his monarch enjoyed. But, like others before him, he paid a ruinous price. He leased a theatre, The Imperial, for Lillie. She insisted on having it refurbished according to her own specifications. It cost Edward untold thousands of pounds to fulfil her wishes. The plays in which Lillie appeared were dismal failures and her relationship with the now much poorer Edward Cohen stuttered to a close. Her theatrical career was also coming to its end.

Lillie was now in her fifties and still handsome, but no one keeps their looks for ever. She had put on weight, her ankles had thickened and her face was becoming fat. The more she persisted in trying to play the young and alluring, gay and sexy mistress of a king the more grotesque she became. She joined the vaudeville circuit in America and appeared on the same bill as acrobats, performing seals, illusionists and chimpanzees. It was a sad and tawdry ending. She was fearful of the future, even though she was very wealthy. She had a husband she did not love and a daughter who would not speak to her. Lady de Bathe she might be, but the number of her worshippers was diminishing. She had become a freak show in a circus.

On 7 May 1910, Lillie was summoned peremptorily from her Newmarket house to Buckingham Palace. King Edward, the greatest benefactor Lillie ever had, was dead and with him went a whole world. Edwardian England with its frivolity, its vice, its dazzling hypocrisy, disappeared almost overnight. Lillie, who had been a denizen of that world, understanding perfectly the mechanisms that made it tick and understanding perfectly, too, how to exploit it to her own advantage, had nowhere to call her home.

She went on another tour of America, in vaudeville. It failed miserably. She also made a film but the camera made her appear exactly what she was: a rather wooden, middle-aged has-been. Lady de Bathe knew it was the end. It was time to leave the stage. Time, indeed, to leave England.

She sold up all her properties and left the bright lights and high society for Monte Carlo where she bought a house that she named, of course, Le Lys. Here she spent her remaining years, surrounded by photographs and portraits of the great, and often regal, characters she had known and laughed with in the high summer of her life when she was beautiful beyond compare and when lords and ladies, poets

and painters, princes and kings danced attendance on her every whim and sang her praises in every corner of the realm. That time was long gone. Most of her friends were dead. Lillie had riches, furs and jewels without number, but they seemed to please her little. Her old age was not a happy time. She was melancholic, introspective, bitter and, above all, lonely. A woman fashioned entirely by a sensual society where novelty is everything, caring for little but glamorous appearances and instant gratification of all desires, is ill-suited to live contentedly through old age. Lillie died on 12 February 1929. Her wish was to be buried in St Saviour's churchyard in her native home of Jersey. You may see her grave, a little to the west of the church, surmounted by a marble bust of her head.

The people of Jersey crowded into the cemetery on a bitterly cold day to see the end of Emily Le Breton. It had been a fabulous career

Right: Marble bust above Lillie's grave. It captures a little of her beauty.

Overleaf: Lillie's final resting-place is in the graveyard of St Saviour's Church, on the high hill overlooking St Helier. Although her daughter, Jeanne-Marie, did not communicate with her for over 25 years, she attended the funeral.

and, in its own terms, mostly successful. She had wanted glamour, fame and fortune. God gave her the beauty and she used it at first artlessly and then with a courtesan's skill, to gain that fame and fortune. She won the love of a prince and, more than that, turned him from a lover to a friend for life. She ran her own theatre company with great success, no mean feat in a world dominated by men. She was not perfect by any manner of means. She was endlessly, and often unattractively, acquisitive. But she was never ever boring and, above all, she survived. The Jersey Lily, in the course of a long career, brought inspiration and excitement, gaiety and joy to thousands upon thousands of people. Not many can claim as much.

A race meeting on Grouville Common. Lillie took time off from her tempestuous theatrical and private life to join the horse-owning fraternity under the name of 'Mr Jersey'. Her horse, Merman, won the Cesarewitch in 1897 and she named her little house in Jersey after him.

6

THE OCCUPATION YEARS

---•---

I saw it from Blanc Pignon on the 28th June. The maid was to take my little girl to the beach but I heard distant bombing and said have a shower instead. Round about six o'clock I was brushing her hair in front of the window and suddenly the three bombs went off over St Helier and we could see the smoke go up. Before I had time to think, the airplane was right in front of us in the field opposite the flats. Two Frenchwomen were digging potatoes and putting them in the barrels. The people in the flats called out 'Fall down, fall down!' and they did and I saw distinctly that the pilot was machine-gunning and I thought he was going to turn on us. I grabbed up the child and ran down the stairs and went to this spot surrounded by granite walls. I swore like never before. The Irish cook did all her Hail Marys.
(Mrs Tottie Resch)

---•---

The Germans were coming. The unthinkable was about to happen: Jersey was to be occupied. No one had believed it would come to this. There had been no attempt to invade the island since the ill-fated Baron de Rullecourt at La Rocque in January 1781. Jersey had escaped any kind of military involvement during the First World War, and confidently expected similar good fortune in the second. Indeed, the tourist industry was advertising the island as a retreat from the trials and tribulations, stresses and strains of warfare. At most, it was fondly thought, Jersey would be used for prisoners-of-war and to provide hospital facilities for personnel wounded in the main European theatre of war. It was a short-lived belief. The Germans swept through the Netherlands, around the Maginot Line and advanced swiftly to the very shores of Normandy. The island boats performed miracles in taking the beaten British soldiery off the French beaches and ferrying them back to safety, but nothing could halt the German advance on to Jersey. A

CHRONOLOGY

1940

24 June	Demilitarisation of Channel Islands.
28 June	German air raid on St Helier kills several people.
1 July	Occupation of Jersey; Erich Gussek, first German commander, arrives.
27 September	First anti-Semitic laws are issued.

1941

17 March	François Scorner, a French boy captured off Guernsey after escaping from France, is executed.
31 August	Black market price for 1 cwt (51 kg) sugar is £50.

1942

6 June	Surrender of all civilian wireless sets is ordered; many are retained at great risk.
15 September	Order to deport non-Jersey-born residents; 1186 people are deported in the following 10 days.

1943

12 January	Second deportation order; 87 people are deported from Jersey.
2 August	Complete ban on fishing.

1944

17 June	Hitler decrees that the Channel Islands must be defended 'to the last'.
1 September	Violations of food regulations are punishable by death.
9 September	End of gas supply.
27 December	First visit of the Red Cross ship SS *Vega* with 750 tons of food.

1945

13 January	No telephone service.
25 January	End of electricity supply.
8 May	The liberation fleet arrives.
9 May	Germans surrender; Jersey is liberated.

message came from George VI to the Bailiffs of Jersey and Guernsey on 24 June 1940.

———————————————————— ● ————————————————————

For strategic reasons it has been found necessary to withdraw the armed forces from the Channel Islands. I deeply regret this necessity and I wish to assure my people in the Islands that in taking this decision my government have not been unmindful of their position. It is in their interest that this step should be taken in the present circumstances.

The long association of the Islands with the Crown and the loyal service the people of the Islands have rendered to my ancestors and myself are guarantees that the link between us will remain unbroken and I know that my people in the Islands will look forward with the same confidence as I do to the day when the resolute fortitude with which we face our present difficulties will reap the reward of victory.

———————————————————— ● ————————————————————

Jersey was to be demilitarised and left undefended. People in their thousands fled in panic from the island on any transport available – steamers, yachts, even filthy old coal-boats. Cattle were abandoned in the fields. Five thousand cats and dogs were destroyed. Homes, cars, belongings, all were left behind as about 13 000 people left everything and fled for dear life before the advancing German powers.

On 1 July German planes flew low over the island and dropped copies of an ultimatum. Unfortunately, it was printed in German and there was no little difficulty in finding someone to translate it into English. Finally, and fortunately, a German-speaking priest from the Jesuit Order of St Helier was found to perform the task. White crosses were to be painted in the centre of the airport and at the harbour. White flags were to be flown from all houses and fortifications as a sign of surrender. Failure to comply with the terms of the ultimatum before 7 a.m. on 2 July would result in further bombardment.

There was no possible way to resist. Furthermore, Alexander Coutanche, who now combined the offices of Bailiff and Lieutenant-Governor of Jersey, had clear and unequivocal instructions from the British Government to offer no resistance whatsoever. White crosses were duly painted in the prescribed places.

In lieu of white flags, of which there was not an over-abundance

Overleaf: St Brelade's Church. It has kept watch over the most lovely St Brelade's Bay since time immemorial.

in Jersey, white towels, sheets, pillow-cases, shirts – even white knickers – were hung from every window. The Germans marched into the island without let or hindrance.

So began the most difficult and tragic period in the island's colourful history. Not that Jersey should have been unaware of German intentions. For some months prior to the outbreak of war, islanders had been delighted to discover that if they wanted domestic servants, hotel workers or nannies they could employ very willing Germans to do the work. It appears not to have struck them as odd that many of these 'servants' were very highly qualified. It's not often you get housekeepers with law degrees or lowly clerks who are skilled engineers. They were spies.

Jersey was the only part of Britain that German forces occupied. Compared to other subject populations, in other occupied zones, the islanders were fairly well treated at first. There was strict rationing of food. A curfew was imposed and it was forbidden to listen to any wireless transmitting stations except those controlled by Germans, but there was no violence towards the civilian population. At this stage, at least, the Occupation was irritating rather than truly oppressive. Cars were commandeered, farmers were forced to change reluctantly from cultivating tomatoes and potatoes to growing cereal, but nobody was shot. People were annoyed, no more than that, when German troops, benefiting from an extremely favourable rate of exchange, bought up all the luxury goods brought to the island in expectation of a bumper holiday season. Captain Erich Gussek, the amiable German commander, soon put a stop to such purchases. He also lifted the ban on listening to BBC broadcasts on the wireless.

The islanders almost visibly relaxed. True, books disliked by the Nazi regime were removed from the public library and burnt. And true, all Jews had to declare themselves and be registered by the German authorities, and all Jewish businesses had to advertise the fact by putting special notices in their windows. However, few Jersey people used the library and even fewer were Jews, so these events caused little resentment or fear. Resistance was token rather than real. V-signs painted on walls, or ribald remarks about Hitler's sexuality describe the extent of it.

There were, however, a suspicious number of aeroplane crashes at the airport, the result of a very clever piece of sabotage. The Germans had retained the services of Charles Roche when they occupied the island. He was in charge of airport maintenance, with

Right and below: German soldiers, by Edmund Blampied. Baron von Aufsess thought he was vulgar; in fact he is one of the greatest artists Jersey has ever produced.

particular responsibility for keeping the grass runways in good order. The intrepid Roche cut the grass to below the required height, which prevented the wheels of incoming aircraft from gaining proper purchase on the ground. They would overshoot the runway or skid, and crash. He managed to get away with this trick for 2 years, but was finally sent to an internment camp in 1942.

Why did the Germans behave so differently in Jersey from the way they behaved everywhere else they occupied? The answer is thought to be that they were conducting a propaganda exercise to show the British that they were not, after all, barbarians intent on pillage and rape but cultured gentlemen of a kindly disposition. If the people of mainland Britain believed this they would be much less inclined to resist to the last, and more inclined to treat with an enemy they regarded as highly civilised and humane.

This may well have been the case. It is also true that, at least in the early stages, the Germans had no need to show the iron fist. The islanders were co-operating very well without the use of force. There was no Maquis in Jersey. There was only the Superior Council under Bailiff Coutanche, which worked closely with the Germans to their mutual advantage and security. But circumstances deteriorated. Captain Gussek may have believed that the war would be over in a matter of months, but this was not to be. The war in the west reached stalemate. Hitler fatally divided his powers and turned on his former ally, Russia. It was strategically an act of monumental stupidity but it gave the western powers a welcome and much-needed respite.

Because of these events in eastern Europe, Jersey got its first glimpse of the true nature of the Third Reich. Workers, mainly Russians, were shipped in by the Todt organisation. They arrived in their hundreds. Transported for days on end across Europe, in dark, dank and insanitary cattle trucks, they were pushed, prodded and beaten to Jersey to help turn the island into a huge fortress. Even now, all these years later, it is nothing so much as a monument to these and other slave workers, a mute testament to their privation and suffering.

Many of the islanders, at great risk to themselves, helped these wretched fellows. Even the ordinary German troops were moved to give them food. They were stopped by their commanders. One woman, then a little girl, told me that, out of pity, people left apples, and perhaps a little bread from their own meagre rations, on a wall by a road used by a gang of slave workers when they returned from

Overleaf: Some of the many fortifications built by the Germans to turn Jersey into a fortress island. In the event, the Allies simply bypassed Jersey.

Above and right: The underground hospital in St Peter's Valley. It is just as the Germans left it in 1945, with wards, officers' quarters and fully equipped operating theatres. There is also an uncompleted section where the conditions under which the Todt workers toiled may easily be imagined.

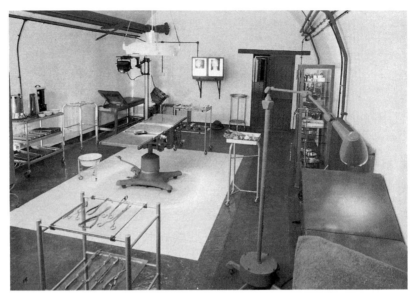

their hard day's labour on the St Ouen sea wall. They had to stop the practice because the workers fought among themselves for the food, which in turn provoked the German guards to assault them with whatever came to hand – a rifle butt or sometimes a shovel. Dr John Lewis, whose book *A Doctor's Occupation* is far and away the best one ever written about the Occupation, tells of a Russian whose arm was severed from his body by the blade of a shovel.

Coutanche, the lieutenant-governor, records how he was outraged by the inhuman treatment of the Russians. He had personally observed them taking the weight off their blistered, bloated and bleeding feet (they had no shoes) by walking on their elbows along the low stone wall by the road. To his everlasting credit, he complained forcefully to Oberst Graf Rudolf von Schmettow, the German commander. To von Schmettow's everlasting shame, nothing was done.

A hammer blow fell on 15 September 1942. In the summer of 1941, the pro-Nazi Shah of Iran had been overthrown and a joint Anglo-Russian force occupied the country. Five hundred Germans stranded there were interned. Hitler was incensed. A means of retaliation lay to hand. There were almost 6000 British people in Jersey, that is, people who lived on the island but had not been born there. Hitler ordered them to be deported.

A notice to this effect was published on 15 September 1942. It was brief and to the point.

NOTICE

By order of higher authorities the following British subjects will be evacuated and transferred to Germany.

A) Persons who have their permanent residence not of the Channel Islands, for instance those who have been caught here by the outbreak of the war.

B) All those men not born on the Channel Islands and 16 to 70 years of age who belong to the English people, together with their families. Detailed instructions will be given by the Feld Kommandantur 515.

Der Feldkommandant
Knackfuss, Oberst.

All the people affected were given the following instructions:

1) You have to appear on the 16.9.42 not later than 4 o'clock at the garage, Weighbridge St Helier, wife and minor children.

2) You have to take with you all papers proving your identity.

3) It is necessary to outfit yourself with warm clothes, strong boots and provisions for two days, meal dishes, drinking bowl and if possible with a blanket.

4) Your luggage must not be heavier than you can carry and must bear a label with your full address.

5) It is further left to you to place ready for each person a trunk packed with clothes to be sent afterwards labelled with full address.

6) It is also left to you to take with you an amount of money not exceeding R.N. 10 in German notes for each person in Reichcredit notes.

7) All valuables (jewels) must be deposited as far as possible with the banks.

8) Keys of the houses are to be handed over to Constables. Should you fail to obey the order sentence by Court martial shall be affected.

Der Feldkommandant
Gez Knackfuss, Oberst.

It was sudden. It was savage. The first deportation under the order was to take place on the following day. This was the severest blow yet to the island community. People who had come to Jersey as babes-in-arms, and had lived there all their lives, were included in the order. The only exceptions were to be on medical grounds, or if the people involved were employed in essential work of some kind.

The misery and despair caused by this action can easily be guessed at. Unable to bear the prospect of deportation, an elderly Englishman and his wife tried to gas themselves. The man succeeded. Leslie Sinel, a journalist on the *Jersey Evening Post*, records in his diary that many English girls married Jerseymen in the hope (never tested) that they would escape the journey to internment camps and an unknown future. Coutanche further records the case of two brothers, one born

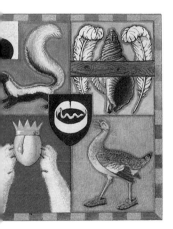

A 'conchy' heraldic symbol attacking conscientious objectors. There was little love lost between the islanders and their unwelcome visitors, and even less between the majority of Jersey folk and the 'conchy'. The 'artist', Rybot, wrote a very fine history of Elizabeth Castle and a much-needed translation of the Chevalier diaries.

An armorial Banner offered by the men of the Fighting Services & mercantile Marine to the Ignoble & Diminutive Confraternity of Contemptible Conchies

Arms Quarterly:—

FIRST. On a field of Blue Funk, a windy Skunk exposed in its true Colours & heading for Cover at the double.

SECOND. Flanked by Plumes of the purest white, a Conch of the deepest Dye, debarred by an inflexible Board proper.

THIRD. Upheld precariously by Ramsay Machiavellian Pussy-Fists, in suspiciously red surroundings, a Bad Egg bearing a False Crown of Martyrdom & exuding a Yellow Streak of foreign Yolk.

FOURTH. On a ground green with poisonous "Weeds", a Ruddy Bustard with cold feet seeking Peas at any Price.

On a Shield of Pretence, a Clerical Collar sheltering a wretched Worm

N.V.L. Rybot
Feb. 1940.

A/1292.

in Jersey and the other in England. Immediately after the birth of the latter, he had been brought to the island where he had stayed all his life. This did not matter to the Germans. Because he had been born in England, he and his family were sent to a German concentration camp. The other brother was allowed to stay. Coutanche objected vigorously to the deportation order, but to no avail. The German commander, Knackfuss, was sympathetic, but the order came direct from Hitler and was personally signed by him. The commander said there was nothing he could do.

On the afternoon of 16 September, the deportees gathered at the Weighbridge in St Helier as they had been commanded to do. They tried to put a brave face on the experience. Large crowds gathered and the Germans, nervous of any kind of demonstration, deployed soldiers armed with rifles and machine-guns to control them. At 9 o'clock precisely, two boats containing 280 islanders including old men, women and children, pulled away from the quay. The crowds gathered on Town Hill heard them singing 'There'll Always be an England' as they slowly disappeared towards Normandy.

The second deportation was on 18 September. Mrs Resch recalls that one fellow due to be sent away had a wife and a mistress. He asked the Germans if he could possibly leave the wife and just take the mistress. They told him he would have to take both.

Even more people turned up to watch this second exodus, to support, cheer and bid emotional farewells to the wretched leavers. The Germans tried to clear the crowds from the streets, but they simply re-formed along Pier Road and up Mount Bingham over-looking the harbour. The first boat left with 430 passengers aboard, and again the onlookers heard the strains of 'There'll Always be an England'. They joined in. A second boat carrying 300 people should have left at the same time but did not do so. German soldiers in Jersey were urgently required in France and there was no other boat to take them. The deportees, granted a brief reprieve, were told to report back to the Weighbridge in 7 days time, which they duly did.

Again there were crowds around the harbour. Groups of young men gathered on Pier Road and sang patriotic songs, which were taken up by others around the town. Things turned ugly. The crowds yelled abuse and gave the V-sign to the soldiers. Schoolboys started playing football with a German helmet. A German officer was knocked unconscious. Soldiers fixed bayonets and drew revolvers. They pursued the rioters and arrested fourteen youths who were

subsequently court-martialled. Fortunately, most were let off lightly but the ringleader was sentenced to 3 years in gaol.

Another order was published in January 1943. It was the last of the deportations, which saw around 1200 people leave the island – more than 200 of them never to return – and which aroused the fiercest protest from Bailiff Coutanche. He and the Superior Council threatened to resign but, in the end, thought better of it.

There has been much criticism of the Jersey Conciliar Government during this time. It has been called collaborationist and quisling. Indeed, many people said so at the time of the Occupation. It is a grey area, and it is a brave and clever man who can tell precisely when enforced co-operation becomes active collaboration. Coutanche's own feelings were that it was to the advantage of the Jersey people to have himself and the Superior Council act as a buffer between them and the German authorities. The alternative was direct rule by the occupying power, and the presumption must be that this form of government would have been far more onerous and arbitrary. Coutanche might not have had much room to manœuvre but he had

a little – and he used it well in the interests of the island. Von Aufsess, the liaison officer between the Germans and the civil authority, confirms very clearly that the need to get Coutanche's assent very often meant that proposed harsh regulations were either softened or withdrawn altogether. The Occupation years might have been even worse had Coutanche and his men not continued in office.

By 1943, the transformation of Jersey from beautiful holiday island to bristling fortress was complete. The work of the Todt organisation remains virtually intact. You will see it everywhere you go. There is no cove, no beach, no cliff-top which does not have bunkers, observation towers and gun emplacements. Even the ancient monuments, Hougue Bie, Mont Orgueil and Elizabeth Castle, have fire towers and command bunkers built on to them. All pointless. Come the Allied landings in June 1944, Jersey was simply bypassed. Except for one quite successful German attack on Granville in Normandy, launched from the island, Jersey served no discernible purpose in the Nazi war effort, apart from providing an inadequate hospital facility for German soldiers injured in the Normandy landings. The underground hospital – originally designed as barracks and workshops – was hardly up to the task of caring for so great a number of wounded. There were shortages of bandages, of disinfectant and, most terrible of all, there was not enough anaesthetic. Serious surgery, including amputation, was carried out on fully conscious men. During these exquisitely painful operations a patient would be held down by four soldiers. As a result, the mortality rate was inevitably very high.

Meanwhile, the living standards of the civilian population continued to decline. Rations were cut periodically until they were only just above starvation level. All essential foodstuffs like potatoes, bread and milk were in very short supply. Meat rations dwindled from 12 ounces (340 g) a week for each adult to 2 ounces (56 g) if you could get it. The provision of gas and electricity became erratic. Supplies of cooking fat, butter, sugar, salt, tea simply ran out. Luxury items such as tobacco and spirits were virtually unobtainable, except in the flourishing black market. Here prices rose steadily until, towards the end of 1944, bars of soap sold for £2 each and 1 lb (450 g) tea sold for £20. There was no petrol for the civilian population. Most cars were commandeered by the Germans although some were artfully hidden in haystacks or barns.

Bicycles became the popular mode of transport, but there were

The bicycle, essential wartime transport. This example is in the Jersey Museum. Tyres were made from old hosepipes, ropes or strips of rubber from lorry or car tyres.

no new tyres to replace those that wore out. Improvisation was the order of the day. Strips were cut off old car and lorry tyres and tied to the rim of the bicyle wheel with wire. A St Lawrence man told me that he packed an old hosepipe with sand and tied that to his wheel. It was, he says, 'bloody uncomfortable but it served'. In the Jersey Museum there are bicycles from this time, equipped with makeshift tyres. There, too, you can see the shoes the islanders were forced to wear. As there was no leather to replace worn-out soles, shoes were repaired with wood making of the footwear a species of clog. One of the most remembered sounds of the Occupation is the sound of these clogs, clattering and reverberating on the streets and pavements.

However, some islanders could obtain pretty much what they pleased, and they were the most despised people in Jersey. They were called 'Jerry bags', a colourful demotic term for a woman who gave sexual favours to German officers in return for food and expensive gifts. They were different from other young Jersey women who became friendly with German soldiers, as was only natural. Dr John Lewis, who should know, estimates that about 100 children of

German origin were born. In most cases, they were the result of loving affairs not conducted for any kind of gain, and most, if not all of them, were absorbed into the community without any fuss or recriminations.

The Jerry bags were different. These women used their undoubted charms cynically to lead a life of luxury and conspicuous indulgence when the rest of the population was suffering extreme deprivation. It must have been galling for Jersey folk who were without transport, heating or light, who lacked adequate food or clothing and could not obtain even basic medicines, to see a well-dressed, well-fed Jerry bag riding like a queen in the back of a German staff car, or marching to the head of a food queue for items people had been waiting hours to buy. Revenge must have been sweet, and it came at the end of the Occupation.

Some of the Jerry bags were shaved, tarred and feathered after the French custom. One notorious woman, after wisely keeping a low profile for some little time after her German lover's departure, thought she would take a walk one quiet afternoon in Howard Davis Park. She was instantly recognised. A mob gathered and chased her round the park, ripping off her clothes in the process. They caught the nearly naked and terrified creature at last, flung her to the ground and poured engine oil all over her. They would probably have murdered her but she managed to tear herself free and ran off. At that juncture, the centeniers came to the rescue. Some of them held off the baying crowd, while others bundled the forlorn woman into a taxi. She applied for, and received, protective custody. Later she was deported to the mainland. Wisely, she never came back. Other Jerry bags, with more sense, quietly slipped out of the island. John Lewis, the good doctor, told me that one particularly beautiful Jerry bag fled to South Africa, where she carried on where she had left off, married an extremely wealthy man and lived out the rest of her days in great luxury.

For the ordinary islander, and for the ordinary German soldier, life was far from luxurious. There were diversions. German military bands played regularly in the Royal Square. Films were shown at the old Forum Cinema, but they were mostly propaganda films of very little interest. The Jersey Amateur Dramatic Society did sterling work, however, putting on whodunits and pantomimes to take people's minds off the increasing difficulties of everyday life. The German troops organised football matches and relay races through St Helier,

As the food shortage grew intense, no farm animal, bird or domestic pet was safe – witness this poor cat. Seagulls were shot out of the air for food.

but these were discontinued when food shortages caused widespread malnutrition.

These shortages, stalemate in the west and the unfolding horrors of the eastern front slowly but surely sapped the morale of the occupying troops. They realised they were on the losing side. They were ragged and desperately hungry, reduced to foraging in the fields and killing household pets for food. Discipline began to break down. There was open criticism of Hitler.

By 1944, the situation was becoming desperate. In his diary, von Aufsess records a request from the German troops for permission to shoot seagulls. There simply was not enough food to sustain either the Germans or the islanders and the black market flourished as never before. In October 1944, the Feld Polizei made a remarkable discovery: a house, belonging to a French doctor, full of black market goods. There were 20 cwt (1020 kg) potatoes, assorted beef, ham, flour and sugar by the sackload. Von Aufsess displayed all the food in a big shop window in St Helier, with notices saying, 'This horde was confiscated from a local resident' and 'Help defeat the black marketeers'. Huge crowds of desperately hungry islanders gathered to gaze longingly at the great pile of food. They stayed mesmerised in front of the window throughout the day and only broke up when darkness fell. The food was taken to the public kitchen to be cooked and distributed. However, it provided but small respite from the increasing deprivations.

Help from outside was needed if famine was to be averted, and that help could only come from one source: the International Red Cross. Bailiff Coutanche begged the German authorities to appeal directly to this body. His efforts were nobly backed up in the House of Lords where Lord Portsea made many impassioned pleas to the British Government to provide Jersey with much-needed relief. It looked as though it would never come.

In the summer of 1944, the bailiff sent a memorandum to the Germans setting out precisely how far the food situation had deteriorated and exactly how long it would be before there was absolutely nothing left. He threatened them with retribution after the war if they allowed the island population to starve to death:

●

It is an undisputed maxim of international law that a military power which in time of war occupies any part of the inhabited territory of an adversary, is bound to provide for the maintenance of the lives of the civilian population. Sooner or later the clash of arms will cease and the powers will meet, not only to consider the means of an enduring peace but also the past judgements on the authorities be they civil or military. Upon whose conceptions of honour, justice and humanity the fate of occupied peoples and places has been temporarily determined. May the insular government be spared the duty of adding to the problems which will face the powers an allegation that by an unjustified prolongation of the siege of Jersey the military representatives of the German government unnecessarily endangered the health and indeed the lives of the people.

———————————————— • ————————————————

Months passed and finally, on 30 December 1944, the Red Cross ship SS *Vega*, carrying 750 tons of food parcels, arrived in Jersey to a tumultuous welcome. It provided much-needed, if temporary, relief.

The essential question was whether the Germans would try and hold the island to the bitter end or surrender peaceably to the Allies. The fate of Jersey hung on the answer. As was to be expected, hardline Nazis were all for a policy of no surrender and there were deadly serious discussions as to the treatment of the civilian population in such a case. The Nazis proposed commandeering all food-stuffs and leaving the islanders to starve. It was a nightmare scenario, and it almost came to pass.

The situation had taken an awful turn for the worse as a result of the von Stauffenberg bomb plot against Hitler in July 1944. It failed and ended with the death by suicide or hanging of all the plotters. Hitler started replacing his top men with hardline Nazis. Graf von Schmettow, commander of the Channel Islands, was replaced by Admiral Huffmeier.

Huffmeier was an extremely dangerous man as far as Jersey was concerned. He was determined to hold out until the end, even though his troops were in no condition to fight effectively for any length of time. He ordered an attack on Granville on the Normandy coast which took the Allies very much by surprise. They had ignored the Channel Islands during the Normandy landings, little expecting any threat from that direction. Huffmeier soon disabused them. The attack was very successful. Much Allied shipping was sunk and, as a matter of military expediency, the Allies turned their attention towards the Channel Islands. If the threat from Jersey had remained, the solution would have been to bomb the island into submission. Inevitably, this would have caused immense damage and colossal loss of life. After 5 years of suffering and travail, it looked as though the islanders might be bombed to death by their friends. It almost came to that. Encouraged by the success of the first mission, Huffmeier planned a second. It took a direct order from his commanding officer, Admiral Dönitz, now the leader of Germany, to stop him. But stop him it did. At 7.14 precisely, on the morning of 9 May 1945, the

Liberation. Late in coming, but none the less welcome, it ended 5 years of occupation which left the island scarred to this day.

instrument of surrender was signed aboard the British warship HMS *Bulldog*.

There was an explosion of joy. The local paper's headline said it all: 'Thank God'. The rejoicing islanders thronged into St Helier. On 10 May the Union Jack was hoisted in the Royal Square. Charles II's Royal Mace, given in gratitude for the islanders granting him refuge, was paraded before the huge crowd. An attempt was made to sing the national anthem, but, as Mr Le Brun who was there told me, hardly anyone could join in 'because of some strange affliction in the throat'.

The Tommies arrived in their hundreds and set about loading German prisoners-of-war into transports, removing mines and hurling the huge guns off the cliffs into the sea. At low water, up by Les Landes, you may see the results of their efforts on the rocks below the gun emplacements. Some Germans were kept in Jersey to help this process of demilitarisation.

As the island slowly returned to normal the entrepreneurial skills of Jerseymen were much in evidence. Many of the cars commandeered by the Germans were to be sold back to the islanders. A man we will call Mr Le Maie did a deal with the Tommies who had been entrusted to look after these vehicles and bought all the distributor caps. The buyers of the cars, whose new purchases were lacking a vital piece of equipment, were forced to obtain the appropriate caps from Mr Le Maie. He described his profit from this venture as 'very reasonable'.

More seriously, those who had fled the island before the Occupation began to return. They must have been shocked by what they found. Their houses were looted, either by the Germans or by persons unknown. Many of their friends and relatives had disappeared, some for ever. The whole appearance of the island had changed. Thousands of trees had been cut down for fuel, including those beautiful, old, evergreen oaks along Victoria Avenue. Everywhere they could see German fortifications. From Gronez in the west to Gorey in the east, the little island had been turned into a mighty fortress.

Much remains of those years. But what remains most of all, in the minds of those who lived through the ordeal, is an abiding sense of outrage and anger at what the Germans did. It was indeed Jersey's darkest hour; the islanders had come so very close to famine and annihilation. It will not soon be forgot.

OCCUPATION TESTIMONY

Desmond McGarry

Desmond McGarry was 11 years old when the Germans occupied Jersey. He later left the island to work in a research and development laboratory in England. He has since returned to Jersey. The following are some of his memories of a childhood spent under German rule.

Slave labourers

I saw many examples of Russian slave labourers. They were pathetically treated. There were camps along Route Orange. One day, a friend and myself were very hungry and decided to go into the fields and pick a few potatoes and boil them up somehow. We were on

Sketches of Todt workers, by Blampied. The Russians were treated extremely badly by their masters and many died.

bicycles with hosepipe tyres, very ramshackle, and got out to Route Orange. We hung on to a German lorry and, as we were doing so, we went into a pot-hole. The potatoes we had picked earlier were in baskets on the front of the bikes and they fell into the road. There was a column of Russian slave labourers going by and they broke ranks – we thought the Germans were going to shoot them, but they didn't. The workers got the potatoes, which were raw, and just gnawed at them because they were so hungry. We ourselves ended up at the camps because of this incident, but the Germans didn't harm us and let us go eventually.

———————— ● ————————

We had a very big garden and a lot of fruit trees. The Russian workers used to go by our road and, of course, my mother and father used to try and slip them an apple or a pear. My mother did this on one occasion and a Russian detached himself somehow or other from the column and gave in exchange an old jacket. It was probably lice-infested, but I kept it and thought it quite an acquisition.

Resisting the Germans
The Germans ran their railway along the road and on to the lawn of the Hotel de Normandy. They used to park the engine there at night-time. My friend and I went along one night and lifted the cover off the gearbox, put a spanner inside and put the cover back. I'm not too sure what happened, but it must have done some damage. We also put a pom-pom shell on the railway line in front of the Omaroo Hotel which was occupied by the Germans.

———————— ● ————————

On one occasion there was a huge explosion and we learnt that the Palace Hotel was being blown up. It was occupied by the Germans. We went up past Victoria College, and were stopped by the German military police who wouldn't let us go any further. Being islanders, we cut across Mr Pallot's field and went to the back near the Palace Hotel where we crouched down and watched all that was going on. There was explosion after explosion. I remember one terrific one when a girder went up into the air. My pal and I crouched by a bank and I heard a thud somewhere near to me. When I looked up, I saw it was a rather battered, silver milk jug. I picked it up – and dropped it immediately because it was so damned hot. It had the crest of the Palace Hotel. We saw bodies being thrown out of the hotel and ammunition going up. The place was pretty well demolished.

Interrogation

Silver Tide was the main Gestapo interrogation place. It was a private house. Some of the personnel from there used to go around in civilian clothes, obviously trying to mingle and overhear conversations. At the age of fourteen I was interrogated at this sinister establishment.

There were two officers there. They interrogated me and had me marched into prison with a German guard on either side. When I got there I saw a cousin of mine, Dennis McLinton, walking up and down in Indian file with other prisoners. As soon as he saw me, he started shouting, 'Hello Des' and all that and the Germans accompanying me gave me very hard looks. They thought that if I knew people in there I should certainly be confined myself. I was shown my brother Patrick, who was then just seventeen. He had contracted yellow jaundice and was terribly ill-nourished and really emaciated. He told me I was going to be taken back to Silver Tide and interrogated that afternoon, and this happened. I was taken into the front room and accused of several things. The Germans made the point that I had been able to see my brother that morning, and said that if I let them have the information they required my brother would be released but I myself would stand trial. They used some persuasion because my teeth were knocked to one side and I lost a tooth.

They told me they knew that Patrick and a friend had gone down to the FB Playing Fields when the Germans had been there on sporting activities. He and a friend had gone into their dressing-room and stolen two Luger pistols.

I think all of us who stole in those days were only souvenir hunters. I don't think anyone had any intention of using the pistols on the Germans. But then, who knows? If you are put in a position where someone is pointing a gun at you, and it's either you or he, perhaps you would use it. However, this never transpired and we personally never killed any Germans.

I was eventually released. The only reason was that the gaol was so full. They put me on parole and gave me time to think things over and come forward with information. But it was only a matter of weeks then before our glorious Liberation.

Wireless sets

When the Germans were rounding people up we decided to hide things like our crystal set in a granite wall. Granite walls are quite thick and this one was anything up to 61 cm [2 ft]. I took away the wooden base of a window and excavated the granite underneath. Then I put back the base and had a sliding door.

When the Germans eventually came for my brother Patrick, they first went to De La Salle College and got my younger brother, who was only about 9 years old at the time. They took him to my house. Patrick was ill in bed at the time, but they searched the house and even pulled up floorboards. Then they went to the building where I'd made my hideout. They searched up there and never found it. If they had done, the punishment would have been severe. Not only did I have a crystal set, I also had a pistol, stick hand-grenades, pom-pom shells and ammunition.

———————— ● ————————

We listened to the BBC a lot. We used to hear Bing Crosby singing 'Don't fence me in' – we were, quite literally, fenced in at the time. We had to be careful. When we listened to the tunes we'd memorise them and, if we went down the street whistling them, we could be pulled in; the Germans used to listen to the broadcasts and would know that we must have been listening. But it was such a consolation to hear the news.

Clothing

For clothes, we managed with stolen German blankets. We made up a home-made dye and dyed them, then we gave them to a friend of ours who had been a tailor in the British Army before the war. He made shorts for me and my brother and a sort of windcheater. Because the material was dyed and fashioned in a certain way, there was little chance of the Germans recognising their blankets. We didn't have shoes. Clogs were made of thick wood with steel plates at the front and back, and strips of German tyre underneath so that even school-boys looked quite tall.

Food

The Red Cross ship, the SS *Vega*, was only able to make five deliveries of prisoner-of-war parcels in 5 years. People of English extraction were deported and they were sent to camps in Germany. They weren't concentration camps. In fact, apart from the terrible business of being separated from their loved ones in Jersey, the people who had been deported were better off foodwise. I understand that some of them had as many as three Red Cross parcels a month. Our last delivery came on our day of Liberation.

The SS *Vega*. This Red Cross ship was the most welcome sight of the war years: it brought food, at last, to the starving islanders.

Opposite to us was a bakery where they used to make bread. It was terrible, because we didn't have bread for a long time and we could smell it being baked. I used to go there with this tall bucket, almost like a milk churn, that opened at the top and was really narrow. I pretended to get hot water, which they allowed us to have, and would come out with the bucket. Then I'd steal a loaf, put it in the bucket and sort of struggle as though I was carrying a lot of water. We'd just tear at that bread – no butter, nothing like that, just as it was – because we were so very hungry.

———— ● ————

Hunger is a terrible thing. You can put up with a lot of other things but hunger – it nearly drives you insane. We had a commander named Huffmeier and he told us he would have us eating grass. Well, I had tried (it sounds untrue) shaving soap. At one time we used to get stuff from France and once there was some shaving soap – I nibbled at that. I remember foaming and being almost sick. I even tried grass. I mean, when a dog is ill it eats grass, it does it good. But this chap vowed that he would have us eating grass.

Liberation

At Liberation the reception of the British troops was beyond belief. We couldn't believe they were here. They were typical of Tommies, getting out their cigarettes and their small rations and giving them to people. But we couldn't understand some of the soldiers. We came

Clutching Red Cross parcels brought by the SS *Vega*, some very happy people rush home to enjoy their first proper food in many months.

to the conclusion that they might be Polish troops serving in the British Army. Actually, it was just that we were unused to hearing strong British regional accents. A very pronounced Yorkshire or Welsh accent was alien to us. We'd become so used to hearing the posh accents on the BBC news that these people seemed unintelligible.

———— ● ————

I looked across and saw the SS *Vega*, the Swedish ship that was instrumental in bringing our last Red Cross parcel consignment. We were so eager to get to it that we went down to the harbour. We ignored the Germans and, with an axe that was always beside the rafts, we cut through the ropes securing a raft. It went into the water and we then jumped on to it. We had a hell of a shock because we went right through the rotten netting at the base of the raft. We then got on land again and made our way round the barbed-wire perimeter fence to where the SS *Vega* was stationed. We had to fight our way

on board, there were so many people there. I think they were attracted by the lovely aroma of fried bacon and sausages. We really had a most marvellous meal.

———————— • ————————

Shortly after Liberation we began to get white bread. This was a great treat. The bread tasted like the finest cake would taste to us now. Eating it was a moment of great joy, the likes of which I have never experienced again.

British troops march along the Esplanade and Victoria Avenue. They stayed to help clear up the island after the Germans had left.

TOTTIE RESCH

Tottie Resch was born in Australia and married to a German. Her husband, who died during the Occupation, was part of the Resch brewing empire. Her daughter is the owner and breeder of Europe's prize cows. Mrs Resch describes some of her experiences during the Occupation.

Encounter

An early encounter with the enemy was at Christmas – they had arrived in July. An air force officer came to the door and wanted to have our little Canadian spruce trees as Christmas trees. I said, 'No, they've taken years to grow.' He said, 'We're going to England. You can plant all the Christmas trees you want.' I said, 'You haven't got to England yet,' and he said, 'We will when Hitler gives the order.' He tried to bargain – money and cigarettes. In the end, we got down to one tree. I said, 'Would you give it to me in writing?' and he drew himself up another 15 cm [6 in] and said, 'Would you doubt the word of a German officer?'

In the New Year, the same officer came back and brought a big box of chocolates from Paris. It hurt me very much to refuse them. And he said, 'You haven't hung out your washing on the Siegfried Line.' My reply was, 'We shall hang it out in *Unter der Linden* [Berlin] before we finish.'

Requisitioning

Eventually there was a knock on the door, and there was a German officer saying he had come to requisition the house. They had already taken our one in St Peter and this was a big shock. He came in and looked around. My husband, who was fifty-eight at the time, asked if they were going to put officers in. He said no, they were going to put in sixty troops. He told us we would have to take everything out, our carpets, furnishings. Well, that was the end of my husband. You hear of people turning white instantly – he completely changed. We went to the next room, which had a little suite of child's furniture. Suddenly the German officer stopped, more or less clicked his heels together, came out and went down the stairs. At the door, he said, 'I will see what I can do,' and put out his hand to shake. Everyone said, 'Don't shake hands with a German,' but in a situation like that you don't refuse. He went away.

We got in touch with our lawyer and told him what had happened. That night, my husband packed a case. He was convinced he would be taken to Germany because Hitler had said that even second generation Germans born outside Germany were still German citizens. His mind went. He thought they would take him away. Three months later my husband died from a stroke – he never recovered from the shock. He was more British than the British.

The baron

I had been out in the pony and trap with my little daughter. I came up the drive and was followed by a car with three German officers. They followed us to the house. I had previously used a lot of electricity

Overleaf: The German section of St Brelade's churchyard during the war. The Germans buried here had died in Normandy and elsewhere, not in Jersey.

boiling water with Friars Balsam for my daughter who had bad asthma. I had had to write a letter explaining why I had used more than my ration, and I thought they might have come about this. I was very nervous with them but they went away. I discovered later that one was Baron von Aufsess [liaison officer between the Germans and the civil authority] and another was a doctor. They came again – it was just out of curiosity. It was bad luck for me, because once the baron had discovered us, I think they put us on their visiting list, like Noirmont Manor, Samarès Manor and Rozel.

———— ● ————

The three Germans came again and wanted me to take them around the garden. They came to an enormous big pine tree and the baron stopped and said, 'Trees are better friends than men.' I said, 'Why?' and he said, 'They don't talk.' When I got one of the other officers alone, I asked what was wrong. He told me that the baron's wife had been arrested and put in a concentration camp. The baron spent 2 years as a prisoner in the United Kingdom.

———— ● ————

I thought von Aufsess was a gentleman. He was a baron. He had an old eleventh-century castle and all the rest of it. He used to look scruffy compared to the other officers – he didn't waste money on his uniforms. But in a book he wrote later, the baron made out my husband had built a folly in the garden – it was there 100 years before. He said he advised me about being a widow – that's completely untrue. He said I showed photographs of my family – that was untrue. He gives the impression he was invited into my house and had drinks – that was untrue. It spoilt my impression of him.

Food
Rations got smaller and smaller. The Germans could get food from Normandy. Civilians couldn't. The Germans allowed a Jerseyman to travel in France to buy food for the black market, for the civilians. By doing that, they didn't have to bother with feeding us.

———— ● ————

Our ration got down to 4 oz [110 g] meat a week, including bone. People did actually die of starvation. The Dean of Jersey had become a good friend. He used to come out to see us sometimes. When these kind of people came I'd try hard to give them a really good meal. I'd give the dean six eggs – and he'd give them to some old man. So I made him promise to eat them himself because he was starving too. I tried to produce food for as many as possible. I had thirty different varieties of beans, over sixty fowls. People would come begging for this and that. I said, 'Pick off the lime flowers to make lime tea, shell beans, you can have all you want – but don't expect us to do the work.' They never came. Everyone wanted something, but they expected it all to be done for them.

———————— ● ————————

One day I had 25 lb [about 11 kg] of black market meat on my kitchen table. I thought that if I got caught with it I would be in a concentration camp. People came because I lived in a big house and I used to buy black market meat to help my neighbours. But the price got too high: I stopped when it went up to 4 shillings a pound [450 g].

———————— ● ————————

We were allowed to have registered pigs. We had two. We'd save everything and anything to try and feed those wretched pigs. One was sent to the abattoir and we got 10 per cent – just about one leg. I had to divide it into thirteen pieces for the people who worked for me – I was giving everyone work to do so that they didn't have to work for the Germans.

After getting a present of some delicious bacon I determined I too was going to have real bacon. The vet found me someone on the other end of the island who would kill our other pig and turn it into four hams and two sides of bacon. He came, and I had to make sure everyone was away and the maid out. I had this awful, big, naked pig hanging up in the laundry. I put the black-out curtains up and locked the doors and got to work with a butcher's saw and Mrs Beeton to carve it up. To turn it into bacon, I had to take it all the way through town in the little cart until we got to a farm where they could cure it. When I went in, there were Germans all over the place. I took a big basin of eggs for the lady.

She showed me this outside kitchen, which all Jersey houses had at one time, with a huge chimney where you could smoke about seven hams. I left the pig there to be cured. I didn't realise what the smell would be and when I went back for it in my cart I wondered how I would get home without being stopped by the military police. As I came down into St Helier it began to rain. It poured down. I'd bought myself a fisherman's sou-wester and had a cover made to go over the cart so that the water couldn't get in. We were the only people on that road, but we got home without being stopped.

I began to worry about what would happen if the inspector came to check up on my registered pig. We managed to get a small replacement and had great fun trying to make it grow quickly – we'd rush to pick up our acorns before the Germans, who were also keeping pigs, could do so. Time went by and an inspector came, a Jerseyman. Someone had informed on me to the Germans, saying I'd had an unregistered pig. He said it was the best pig he'd seen in many a day and that I should send it in the following week! That pig was 9 months old. It should have been 2 years old.

Afterwards, the Germans offered me another one. I said I could only have registered pigs but they said, 'Ours aren't registered.' So we started again – when people are dying through lack of food, you take any risk. My life was made up of ways and means of finding and producing food.

German disillusionment

A German officer came into the garden looking for a footpath shown on a map. As I showed him the way out he came to the chickens and went, 'Put, put, put, put, put.' My little daughter said, 'Mummy, I think he's Colonel "Put Put".' So that was his nickname. One night, later on, he came knocking at the door reeking of drink. I'd discovered during his first visit that he was a judge, so I was angry that he'd turned up like that at night-time. I said, 'If you're looking for a woman, go to the streets of St Helier,' and slammed the door in his face. The next day, I rang up and asked for a notice on my gate in German because of a drunken soldier. They put one up. (Other large gardens had such notices.)

One day he appeared again. I was rude to him, saying, 'They haven't sent you to the Russian front yet, but I hope it won't be long.' He went away and we didn't think of him for a long time.

Then one day, we were in the trap when somebody pressed the splash-boards down from the back. It was 'Put Put'. But I saw he had been demoted. Everything had gone – his Iron Cross, everything. I asked what had happened, but he didn't say a word, just dropped back. I made it my business to find out: he had been in the officers' mess in the Pomme d'Or Hotel and taken out his pistol and fired a shot straight through Hitler's portrait. So we were sorry we had been rude to him. We never saw or heard of him again.

German soldier walking along the quayside in the shadow of instantly recognisable Gorey Castle.

VICTIMS OF THE OCCUPATION

Some commentators have pretended that the German Occupation of Jersey was rather a pleasant affair. That the people did not suffer unduly, and certainly not as much as those in other occupied zones. But Jersey suffered enough. People were deported. People did die. Lives were blighted, if not destroyed for ever, during the 5 years the Germans were there. These are just some of the men and women who suffered, many mortally, at this time.

Andre, André – Arrested 1943. Taken from Jersey for forced labour, escaped and joined the Free French Air Force.

Cohu, Clifford (Canon) – Sentenced to 3 years for spreading BBC news. Died in Spergau concentration camp.

Dauny – Information sought. In Villeneuve St George's Prison, 1943.

Delauney, Geoffrey – Insulted a German. Sent to Villeneuve St George's Prison. Survived.

Dimmery, A. – Information sought.

Faramus, Charles – Arrested 1941. Some time at Buchenwald. Survived.

Fox, George – Arrested 1943. Died 11 March 1945, at Naumberg/Salle, Germany.

Gallichan, George – Arrested 1942 for circulating a document against German orders. Sent to Dijon Prison. Survived.

Gallichan, Herbert (brother of George) – Sent to Wolfenbüttel concentration camp. Survived.

Gould, Louisa, Mrs – Arrested for harbouring a Russian prisoner. Died at Ravensbrück concentration camp.

Gould, Maurice – Arrested 1942. Died at Wittlich camp in Germany, 1943.

Gourdan, Paul – Sentenced 1942. Went to Caen, Dijon, Poland and 13 months in Buchenwald. Survived.

Green, Stanley – Sentenced for radio offence. Went to Fresnes, Belsen and transferred to Laufen. Survived.

Hassell, Peter – Sentenced in 1942 with M. Gould. Survived.

Houillebecq, James, aged 17 – Weapons offence. Died in Neuengamme concentration camp.

Kinnaird, Lillian, Mrs – Sentenced with her sister Kathleen Le

Normand to 9 months in Caen Prison for making V-signs. Survived.

Le Druillenec, Harold – Sentenced for harbouring escaped Russian pilot. Sent to Neuengamme, Wilhelmshaven and Belsen. Survived.

Le Normand, Kathleen – Sentenced with Mrs Kinnaird to 9 months in Caen Prison. Survived.

Le Villio, Frank, aged 18 – Last seen at Neuengamme concentration camp.

Malherbe, Madame – French lady living in Jersey. Sentenced to death with Madame Schwob for distributing anti-German propaganda. Reprieved.

Marsh, William – Died of ill-treatment in Germany on 3 March 1945.

Nicolle, John W – Sentenced 1943 to 2 years for spreading BBC news. Died in a camp in Dortmund, Germany, 1944.

Ogier (Advocate) – Sentenced 1942 for defamatory remarks against Germans. Died in a German camp, 1943.

Ogier (son of above) – Survived.

Page, Frederick – Sentenced 1943. Died of ill-treatment at Naumberg/Salle, Germany, September 1944.

Painter, Clarence, snr.

Painter, (Peter) C, jnr – Arrested 1943. Sent with his father via the notorious Cherche Midi prison to Natzweiler, Silesia, then to Krupp factory. Both died.

Paisnel, Emile J – Sentenced 1944. Died of ill-treatment at Naumberg/Salle, Germany, September 1944.

Pitolet, Miss – Sent to a French prison for harbouring an escaped Russian. Survived.

Queree, Clifford – Sentenced 1943. Died of ill-treatment, 1945.

Ross, Edward O.

Ross, Nan, Mrs – Sentenced 1942 for possessing a radio and assisting Russian and Polish prisoners. Sent to France and separated. Both survived.

Schwob, Madame – Sentenced to death with Madame Malherbe for distributing anti-German propaganda. Reprieved.

Soyer, Jack – Sentenced 1943 for a radio offence. Escaped in France and died fighting for the Maquis, 29 July 1944.

Stephan, Louis – French resident taken from Jersey for forced labour in 1943 with A. André. Escaped and joined the French Army.

Tierney, Joseph – Sentenced to 2 years for spreading BBC news. Died of ill-treatment in Celle, Germany, 1945.

7

JERSEY KILLINGS

Jersey is a holiday island of extreme beauty, and its crime rate is the same as that of any average seaside town. That is to say, quite low. The great majority of offences have to do with drink – young men fighting outside pubs or discothèques, causing affray and riot and assaulting each other or the hard-pressed constabulary. There is too, and more seriously, a drugs problem. Smack, cannabis and ecstasy are becoming increasingly available, even to schoolchildren. Opportunist petty theft, particularly in summer, is rife as may be expected in a resort crowded with thousands of happy holiday-makers careless of their possessions. Serious robbery is extremely rare, for the simple reason that Jersey is surrounded by sea. If you steal the stuff, how do you get it off the island, when all the exits – airport, harbour and marinas – can be very well monitored? It is well nigh impossible.

Serious crime in Jersey therefore figures very little in the headlines of the local Press, and really serious crime such as murder hardly ever. It was not always so. Throughout history, Jersey has been no stranger to killings of the most brutal kind. But it has taken our own twentieth century to produce the most bizarre, savage and inexplicable murder of all.

JEHANNET DE ST MARTIN

The first Jersey murder we know of is recorded in a Latin manuscript of about 1540.

In the mid-fourteenth century there dwelt in Jersey the rich and kindly Philippe de Barentin, Seigneur of Rozel Manor. He was also Seigneur of Samarès Manor and three other manors, as well as two in England. His great wealth derived from the signal service his ancestors had done the King of England, who had made the family by way of reward very wealthy. At the time of which we speak, the Barentin family had lived in Jersey for over 100 years.

Philippe was very different from his immediate ancestors. They had been arrogant, high-handed aristocrats, not at all averse to exercising every right they could possibly lay claim to. He, on the other hand, was a more gentle soul who delighted in tending the beautiful gardens of Rozel Manor, or fishing off the island's rocky coasts. He had two fine sons, Gilbert and Philippe, by his wife Mabelle. She must have been in her mid-thirties in 1362. One son was 18 years old and the other seventeen.

In that tragic year, according to the sixteenth-century chronicler, Mabelle told her two sons, but not her husband, that a terrible insult had been offered her: 'Jehannet de St Martin has called me an adultress. Avenge this insult on your mother. I would such slanderers had their tongues torn out by the roots.' Jehannet de St Martin was possibly the son of their neighbour, the Seigneur of Trinity, who became Bailiff of Jersey in 1370.

The accusation of adultery was a mortal insult and not to be borne. The chronicler continues the story: 'The sons in fury laid an ambush and set a boy to whistle a warning when de St Martin came near. When he came, they seized him and tore out his tongue where today stands the cross called the Cross of Jehannet, about 400 yards from St Martin's Church as one goes towards Trinity. This cross was placed there in memory of the crime.'

News of the outrage spread like wildfire. The hue and cry was raised and the two sons fled for dear life to France. One was almost immediately captured and ended his short life dangling from a gibbet. The other, more fortunate, made good his escape to Rouen, where he lived all the rest of his days in peace. De Barentins were still to be found in that beautiful city as late as the sixteenth century.

The gentle Philippe de Barentin was amazed and horrified at his sons' outrageous act. He found he could no longer bear to live on the island, and left Jersey to live for ever in England, away from the scene of the tragedy.

There is a curious postscript to this story of Jersey's first known murder. Philippe left his island manors in the hands of two attorneys, giving them instructions that they should sell them as soon as possible. However, Philippe's sister's son was the rector of St Brelade and this gentleman had more than a passing interest in the projected sale. In true Jersey fashion, he objected to de Barentin's great properties going

Overleaf: St Brelade's Bay. This is the view from the church where Philippe de Barentin's brother-in-law was rector at the time of Jersey's first recorded murder.

out of the family. He objected with such fervour that he tried to get Philippe declared a leper. If he succeeded in this endeavour, his uncle would be wrapped in a shroud, placed in a coffin and have the burial service read over him. As far as the law was concerned, Philippe de Barentin would cease to exist. He would be dead. He would spend the rest of his days in ditches and byways, shunned by the world.

The rector failed in this attempt, though it has been proved that there had once been leprosy in the de Barentin family. Meanwhile, the attorneys could find no buyer for the manors and suggested that they themselves should buy the estate and give Philippe £200 a year during his lifetime. Philippe accepted this proposal but his nephew, the rector of St Brelade, was not yet finished. He challenged Philippe's right to dispose of his property to men who were of Breton origin but who had not obtained permission as aliens to buy property in Jersey. Then as now, the island's property laws were tightly controlled. The action went on for years. The law was obscure, the arguments tortuous, but Philippe eventually won the day. The manors were sold to the two lawyers. One got Samarès and all de Barentin's manors to the south. The other, a Raoul Lempriere, got Rozel manor. He was the first of a long line of Lemprieres who have fluctuatingly occupied Rozel right down to the present day.

GEORGE LE CRONIER

Murder on the island has almost always been an exceedingly bloody affair. Records show that Jersey killers seldom resort to poison, suffocation or strangulation. It is always the knife, the hammer or the ubiquitous blunt instrument that is used to stab, cut, smash and batter victims to their untimely deaths. Wherever you look in the island's history, this is found to be so. The case of poor Centenier George Le Cronier, fatally stabbed on Friday, 27 February 1846, is an example.

In the course of his duties he had gone to Mulberry Cottage, described thus by a local journalist:

---●---

The appearance is somewhat forbidding, two large double iron gates and a wall some twelve foot high topped with broken bottles hide the house from passers-by. The windows in part of the house are shuttered. These are closed and exclude the sunlight. Inside amongst other rooms there is a beautifully furnished ballroom.

---●---

Mulberry Cottage was a very expensive, luxuriously appointed brothel in St Helier. There had been continuing complaints of rowdy and riotous behaviour in and around this house of ill-repute and the authorities belatedly took it upon themselves to do something about it. The madame, called Marie Le Gendre, was outside her establishment when she saw Le Cronier approach together with his diminutive helper, Henry Luce Manuel. She had no cause to like the centenier. A few days before he had removed all her girls to prison, depriving her of a very lucrative income. 'Look, the old bugger is coming!' she exclaimed, and went back into Mulberry Cottage. Le Cronier followed. In a small drawing-room, the confrontation took place. Le Cronier threatened to arrest Marie if she would not consent to appear in court the following day. An argument ensued and suddenly Marie snatched a carving knife from the table behind her and stabbed the unfortunate policeman in the stomach, accompanying her action with a triumphant 'La!'.

Little Manuel ran into the street calling for help. Marie fled to a nearby shop on the corner of Gloucester Street. Le Cronier himself then staggered to the front door saying, 'I am stabbed, I am stabbed.' He was in terrible agony and was removed gently to a house in Sand Street. Here he was laid on a sofa and two doctors, Fixott and Quesnell, were soon in attendance. But it was all to no avail: Marie had done her work too well. The blade of her knife had penetrated the large intestine and there was more than $2\frac{1}{2}$ pints (1.5 litres) of blood in the abdominal cavity. He was taken on a final journey to his house in Broad Street where he died in agony the next day.

By the skilful defence of Advocate Hammond, she was not found guilty of first degree murder, which would inevitably have meant hanging, but of a lesser crime, curiously known as voluntary homicide. A species of manslaughter, it carried a much lesser sentence. Marie was condemned to deportation for the term of her natural life, and her property and effects became forfeit to the crown. She made a grand farewell appearance, dressed as if for a royal visit. As the *Great Western* with her on board slipped away from Jersey, she waved a white handkerchief to the crowds on the dockside.

———————— ● ————————

There are very few murders nowadays in Jersey, but this does not make them any the less appalling when they do occur. What follows is an unvarnished, absolutely factual account, in as much detail as is available to the public, of a murder much worse than any that have occurred in living memory – and for which no one has ever been brought to trial.

THE NEWALLS

Nicholas Park Newall was a well-built, 1.8 metre (6-foot) man. He was 56 years old. Nicholas Newall was killed standing in front of the fireplace in his living-room at 9 Clos de L'Atlantique. There was a period of sustained violence, he was attacked with a remarkable degree of ferocity and probably hit with mortal force about the head more than once with a heavy weapon of some kind. The blood from the wounds sprayed in an arc 1.2 metres (4 feet) wide, up as far as the ceiling, on the wall immediately behind him. He then fell to the floor in front of the fire where he lay for some time, long enough to lose a great quantity of blood which soaked through the carpet, through the underlay into the floor beneath.

Elizabeth Newall, attractive, red-haired wife of Nicholas, was a physically fit, well-built, sometime physical education teacher. She was 48 years old. She was killed in her own bedroom at the end of the hallway. The blood was again sprayed liberally to a considerable height, consistent with garotting. Specks of blood were found on the bedside lamp. Again the body had lain on the floor for some little time. Time enough for a large quantity of blood to soak through the carpet, through the underlay to the parquet floor beneath. From the disposition of the blood, it is assumed she was killed on her knees. The bodies have disappeared. They were disposed of – they have never been found. The killer, or killers, have never been charged. These events took place over 4 years ago, sometime in the week beginning 11 October 1987.

Nicholas and Elizabeth Newall were, according to their great friends, David and Maureen Ellam, lovers of life. They were both

The ill-fated Newalls, Nicholas and Elizabeth, who lived for life and for each other. Their bodies have never been found. Their killer or killers are free.

school teachers who had met at university. Twenty years ago they had upped sticks and set sail in their yacht with their two young sons, Roderick and Mark, bound for a new life in the sun and surf of the West Indies. On the way, they stopped off in Jersey and, like many people before and since, fell in love with this rather beautiful island and decided to stay. Nicholas taught at several schools on the island over the years. Elizabeth was a supply teacher and together they led, at least to all outward appearances, a happy and blameless life. Nicholas was, it is true, a somewhat pompous fellow who carried a superior, pedagogic attitude into unsuitable places outside the school. But according to his friends both in Spain and in Jersey, behind the somewhat arrogant exterior was a simple, often kind indeed lovable, man. He was inclined to be lazy and was by no means practical. As David Ellam remarked, Nicholas could not knock in two nails or put in two screws without difficulty. But he could get in his boat and sail clear across to the other side of the world if he felt like it. It is true that he had a slight but recurring illness, thought to be a species of viral infection, which sometimes incapacitated him for days at a time and which led to his early retirement from teaching at the age of 52. But that did not seem to diminish his love of life to any significant degree. Besides, just before that October of 1987, he had had tests in a London hospital which had resulted in his being given a clean bill of health. There was nothing wrong with him. He could look forward to a long and happy retirement.

Elizabeth Newall was a much more vibrant personality, like an overgrown schoolgirl. She was a 'jolly hockey sticks' lady, very noisy, very sociable and always on the phone, particularly to her great friend Maureen Ellam. She was not a tidy person by any manner of means and had little interest in household chores, being essentially an outdoor type, most happy playing tennis, swimming or yachting with her husband. They were a happy couple. More than that, they were very, very close. They did everything together and went everywhere together. They appeared to love each other to the exclusion of almost everything else in the world.

They were not exceedingly rich, but they were comfortably well off. They sent their two sons, Roderick, the elder, and Mark to school in England, to the prestigious Radley College. They bought a house in Jersey, perched on a hill looking across the little beach of Grève de Lecq and out towards the shark-toothed rocks of the Paternosters and the island of Sark. It was called, aptly enough, The Crows Nest and it was the family home of the Newalls – Nicholas, Elizabeth, Roderick and Mark – until 1987 when they moved to the bungalow in Clos de L'Atlantique. David and Maureen Ellam moved into The Crows Nest and became, in a short space of time, fast friends of Elizabeth and Nicholas – indeed, their best and closest friends in the island. As David Ellam says, 'They were fabulous people to spend time with. It's very difficult to get four people who all get on together and we did. Though we were all different in many ways, we all clicked as a foursome and it was a super relationship.'

The bungalow at Clos de L'Atlantique by La Pulente in St Brelade is a modest little building. It is one of a number of frankly rather ordinary dwellings, the views to the sea obstructed by other identical properties or the trees that line the small road to the Atlantic Hotel which is immediately to the north of the estate. It is not, as some

The Newall brothers – Roderick, the elder (*above*), a soldier at the time of his parents' disappearance, and Mark (*above right*), a fund manager. They are as mystified as we all are.

newspaper articles have intimated, a luxurious bungalow worth hundreds of thousands of pounds, rather the reverse. Nor, as has been falsely reported, were the Newalls fabulously wealthy. They were certainly not wealthy by Jersey standards. The island makes a very good living from importing multimillionaires, who often live in great, and often greatly vulgar, splendour in very large houses.

The Newalls were modestly well off and nothing more. It is true that Nicholas Newall was a Lloyd's underwriter. To become that, he would have needed £250 000 in disposable assets. Nicholas must have had that amount at least. Moreover, the couple had recently bought a villa in Javea in Spain, but again, despite tabloid reports to the contrary, by no possible stretch of the imagination can this be described as luxurious or opulent. According to the Newalls' friends, the Matthews, who were their near neighbours in Spain, it is very far from being grand. Though it does have a small swimming pool, it is worth at present prices between £60 000 and £70 000. The Newalls' yacht, which Roderick, the elder brother, is, at the time of writing, sailing round the Falklands, is likewise no grand floating gin-palace. It is a modest, workaday affair worth, I am told on good authority, about £25 000. In short, although Nicholas and Elizabeth were not exactly poor, they were certainly not tremendously wealthy. Their chief source of income was investments. They were very careful to avoid unnecessary expenditure. Nicholas had handed over a large part of the management of his financial affairs to the younger son, Mark, who is a fund manager.

That year of 1987, their financial state seemed set to improve dramatically – an aged uncle, Kenneth Newall, who was in his seventies and who lived just across the water in Sark, had decided to make a pre-decease bequest to Nicholas Newall and to his twin brother, Stephen Newall. It is thought that the money so willed, and to Nicholas, amounted to £500 000. It is impossible to ascertain whether this sum was paid over. Kenneth Newall died soon after Nicholas and Elizabeth on 21 November 1987.

At the end of August that year, the Newalls returned to Jersey from Spain and, on 10 September, went to visit Uncle Kenneth in Sark. They left the island on 14 September. They visited the mainland on 24 September and spent some time in London with Elizabeth's sister, Nan Clark, and her husband Alister. The Newalls then went to Scotland to visit other members of their families. On 6 October they were back on the island. This time for good.

It was Elizabeth's birthday on 15 October. She would be forty-eight. Their two sons Roderick, 22 years old, a lieutenant in the Royal Green Jackets in Winchester, and 20-year-old Mark, the fund manager, arrived unexpectedly on the evening of Friday 9 October, Roderick at 8 o'clock, Mark at 8.30. On the morning of 10 October, at 10 o'clock, Elizabeth and Nicholas went round to The Crows Nest. As chance would have it, it was also Maureen Ellam's birthday that week. The Newalls did not mean to stay long as their sons were to visit them. In the event, they got chatting and stayed 2 hours. Maureen Ellam remembers thinking that there was something distressing them both. They had not fallen out, but something was upsetting them. Elizabeth said that they would be spending more and more time on the island. Maureen did not ask why. Instead, she made a flippant remark about how if that was so, they could have two dinner parties

The two Newall houses. The modest bungalow in Jersey (*above*) and (*below*) the small, and also modest, villa in Spain.

a week – one at The Crows Nest, one at Clos de L'Atlantique. Nicholas and Elizabeth left at noon and returned to the bungalow.

At 1 o'clock, Nicholas went with the younger son, Mark, to pick up a hire van. Mark had just bought a house at Noirmont, a little down the road from his parents, and needed the vehicle to transport furniture from his previous lodgings in St John to his new home. The whole family then lunched together at the bungalow.

At around 3 o'clock, Mark and Roderick left, planning to meet up with their parents later at about 7.30 before going on to a local restaurant, The Sea Crest, at Petit Port for a celebratory dinner. In the evening, Mark's car would not start so he drove the hire van from his house in Noirmont to Clos de L'Atlantique. Before going to the restaurant, they had a bottle of champagne. Mark (who drinks very little and then only vodka) refrained and drove the rest of the family to the restaurant, and back again at around midnight after a splendid champagne and lobster dinner. When they got home, the drinking members of the family tucked into an 18-year-old Macallan malt whisky. At around 2.30 in the morning, though no one was taking particular notice of the time, the two brothers left in the van to go and sleep in Mark's Noirmont house. It was a moonlit night. They returned at 8.30 the following morning for breakfast with their parents.

At 8.45 on the morning of 11 October, Maureen Ellam left The Crows Nest to collect her brother from the airport. On her way there she called in to Clos de L'Atlantique. She had received about ten bouquets for her birthday and thought it would be nice to give Elizabeth one of them. She did not expect to see the Newalls as it was quite early, and an unsociable time of the day. The intention was to leave on the doorstep the flowers, a plant Elizabeth had forgotten on the Saturday and a mosquito-killer Nicholas had lent her a few weeks before. Maureen put the bouquet on the doorstep, rang the bell, not really expecting to see anyone, and turned back to her car. Roderick came to the door and some remarks were passed about the young being up before the old. Roderick said his parents were still asleep. Maureen said, 'Still asleep? Lay these (flowers) on her bed. When she opens her eyes, she'll think she's dead.'

Maureen Ellam left for the airport and the two boys stayed for lunch – scampi provençale – with their mother and father. At about 3 o'clock they drove over to Mark's home in Noirmont to pick up his car. The hired van was returned to Falles Garage. Mark said that

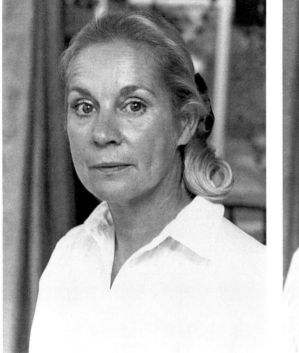

Maureen and David Ellam. The Newalls' greatest friends in Jersey, they consequently feel their loss the most.

he dropped Roderick off at the airport and returned to his house to pick up some baggage before going to the airport himself. Roderick left for Gatwick at 5.45 and Mark flew out of Jersey at about 6.30. Mark could not get his car, a new Toyota MR2 sports model, on the ferry that day so he left it in the airport car park. They had left their parents enjoying a typically quiet Sunday in the seeming security of their own home. The two sons were the last people ever to see Nicholas or Elizabeth Newall.

Maureen Ellam was surprised that Elizabeth, a compulsive phone user, didn't call her later that Sunday. Nor did she phone during Monday 12 October. David Ellam took Maureen's brother back to the airport at 7 o'clock on that day and, roundabout that time, Maureen rang the Newalls. There was no reply. All through Tuesday, repeated calls to Clos de L'Atlantique went unanswered. It was the same on Wednesday. Maureen Ellam thought the couple might have gone to see Kenneth Newall again in Sark. But Thursday, which was Elizabeth's forty-eighth birthday, came and went and still there was no sign, even though the two couples had booked to go to Victoria's – an upmarket restaurant in St Helier – for dinner. The Newalls kept none of their appointments for that week.

On the night of Thursday 15 October, a great storm broke across Jersey, causing massive ruin and devastation and bringing the entire island to a complete standstill. Hundreds of trees were ripped up by the roots and flung across the roads, fields and headlands. The hurricane force winds ripped roofs from exposed houses and brought even sturdy granite walls tumbling down. Miraculously, no one was killed in Jersey, but the life of the island was completely disrupted. Even now, the evidence of that terrible night is everywhere to see. Maureen Ellam, anxious for her friends' safety, tried to ring Sark where she thought the Newalls might be, but all the lines were down. There was no help in that direction. On Friday night, Elizabeth and Nicholas were due at the Ellams for dinner. They didn't come. The Ellams assumed they had been prevented from coming by storm damage and that they couldn't get in touch because of the breakdown in the communications system. Saturday came, still no sign.

Maureen Ellam managed to ring the Newalls' next-door neighbour, Mitchell Shearer at 8, Clos de L'Atlantique, and asked him if he had seen Elizabeth or Nicholas. He said he had not seen them at all during the previous week, and reported that the storm had torn a hole in the Newalls' roof and that the car was parked outside and hadn't moved for the entire week. Where could they have gone without their car? Maureen Ellam asked Mr Shearer to go round to the Newalls' bungalow to see if anybody was home. He duly knocked on the front door and on the windows. There was no reply. He jumped over the back wall and observed that the sliding verandah doors, leading on to the garden, were open. He entered the house, after calling a friend who was staying with him. There was nobody at home. The first thing that struck him on entering was the heat, which was terrific. Towards the utility room in the back he saw mail – some 5 days old – lying on the floor. The lounge was quite orderly, the kitchen had dishes lying around. Nicholas and Elizabeth's bedroom at the end of the bungalow was untidy. Clothes were falling out of drawers and the bed was apparently unmade, but there seemed to be nothing out of the ordinary, no obvious sign of a fight or a struggle.

David Ellam, meanwhile, was on his way to Clos de L'Atlantique from Grève de Lecq. He drove down to the Five Mile Beach and along to the foot of La Pulente Hill leading up to the Newalls' home. He could drive no further; the road had been blocked by the storm. He left the car and walked the rest of the way up to the bungalow and let himself in. There was a big heap of mail on the floor, which he picked up and put on the table. David discovered that the thermostat control had been overridden and the central heating had been left permanently on high. The flowers that Maureen had delivered on the morning of 11 October were in a vase on the sideboard, the wrapper for the flowers was on the floor. The place was tidy. David Ellam, from what he knew of the Newalls' habits, thought it was perhaps over-tidy.

The Ellams contacted Roderick and Mark, voicing their fears about the Newalls' welfare. Roderick returned to the island on Sunday 18 October. Roderick, David and Maureen went over to the house looking for any clues as to where the couple had been. David saw some stains on the carpet in the master bedroom. Maureen said Nick must have spilt a cup of tea that he was bringing to his wife. David was surprised at the lack of newspapers, for Nicholas unfailingly went out on his scooter twice a day during the week to collect not just one, but two or three, of the quality newspapers. He never had them delivered; he always got them himself. On Sundays, he would invariably buy three or four of the upmarket newspapers, but David only saw one section of the *Sunday Times* in the sitting-room. Roderick later said that he had taken the Sunday newspapers off to the plane with him that afternoon. There were no other newspapers dated after 11 October. There was a *Jersey Evening Post* dated 10 October in the waste-paper bin. They inspected the unopened mail. There were birthday cards, circulars, bills and two letters both postmarked 10 October. Roderick was as perplexed as the Ellams and had no idea where his parents might have gone. It was decided to inform the police. Mark arrived back in the island later that day.

At first, the police treated it as a missing persons inquiry, but it soon became clear to them that there was a lot more to this case than at first appeared. Minute quantities of blood, little specks almost invisible to the naked eye, were discovered in certain areas of the house. An incident room was quickly set up from 20 October. A Home Office scientist from the Forensic Centre at Aldermaston, Dr David Northcott, was called in to carry out a complete and thorough examination of the house, collect evidence and advise the police on the implications of what he found. What he found, early in November, led to the missing persons inquiry turning into a murder hunt.

In the sitting-room or the lounge, was found a large quantity of blood that had soaked through the carpet to the floor beneath. There had also been blood splashed on the wall above the fireplace. This

Overleaf: The search for the Newalls' bodies. Intense and persistent, it was to no avail.

227

blood was identified as in all probability belonging to Nicholas Newall. It was the same group as that of his twin brother, Stephen – twins invariably have the same blood group. In the bedroom, more blood was discovered. What Maureen Ellam had taken to be a tea stain was, in fact, blood – a lot of it which, as in the sitting-room, had soaked through the carpet to the floor beneath. This blood was identified as being the same group as Mrs Newall's. It is assumed that Nicholas and Elizabeth were murdered sometime between 11 and 17 October 1987, victims of an episode of sustained violence.

Further, a determined attempt had been made to clean the house up; the carpets and the walls had been washed or scrubbed. It is probable that the duvet in Elizabeth and Nicholas' bedroom had been crudely washed and put back on the bed wet. The heating had been turned up to its full extent to help dry out the building. A rug and some books from the sitting-room were missing. Strangest of all, the only clothes that appeared to be missing from the couple's wardrobe were Nicholas' blue suit with the faint check and Elizabeth's high-necked cream blouse with frills on the cuffs and her red or orange skirt. They are thought to have been the same clothes they were wearing during their dinner with Mark and Roderick at The Sea Crest on the night of 10 October. Mark said that when he and his brother left for the airport on the afternoon of Sunday 11 October his parents were wearing casual clothes.

Suspicions of foul play grew. Intensive searching of the island began, involving hundreds of officers. La Pulente, the area immediately around Clos de L'Atlantique, was, of course, searched very carefully indeed but yielded nothing. The Noirmont area was also thoroughly searched, as were Portelet Common, Beauport, Ouaisne Bay, Sorrel Point and the area round the firing range at Crabbe, just to the east of Grève de Lecq. Using a mechanical digger, officers searched through rubbish and debris at La Saline on the north of the island. The main heap of refuse at La Saline is full of the rotting carcasses of dead cats and dogs dumped there by their owners. It was an unpleasant task and, again, nothing was found.

The search of other dumps, septic tanks, cesspits and bore-holes on the island also failed to produce any evidence as to the whereabouts of the Newalls' bodies. Dogs from the Yorkshire force which had been used in the Moors Murder investigation, were brought across to help in the search as were dogs from the Bolton force, capable of detecting decomposing bodies to a considerable depth in the earth.

Specially trained dogs helped in the search. They are skilled in finding buried bodies – but were unsuccessful on this occasion.

Heat-seeking devices were employed. A radar-like device which could detect bodies under the ground was also brought in, again with no result. Helicopters from France were used to conduct aerial searches. Again, there was no success.

A brand-new spade was discovered on the south coast. Further investigation revealed this to be part of a large cash purchase of tools worth £103, made on the morning of 10 October from Normans, a St Helier's hardware store. The sale included a saw, a pickaxe, two large tarpaulins each 3.6 metres [12 foot] square – one green and one blue – plastic sacks, lamps and scalpels. All of these items could be used in the disposal of two bodies. Despite widespread appeals, broadcast through the media, the purchaser of these goods has never been found. No description of him exists beyond that he was tall and Germanic-looking.

A hundred yards up the coast path from The Crows Nest, at the point where it joins a small metalled road, the remains of a bonfire were found. In the ashes were discovered a number of personal items which belonged to Elizabeth and Nicholas dated from after their move from The Crows Nest. In other words, the items had somehow been brought from Clos de L'Atlantique, all the way over to Grève de Lecq. They included Nicholas Newall's glasses, the remains of a carpet-cleaner container with a brush attached to it, a powder compact and a small handbag containing money all belonging to Elizabeth Newall. Grève de Lecq was thoroughly searched – a whole headland was burned off – nothing more was found.

The island was abuzz with rumours. Everyone had their own theory to explain the disappearance of the couple. There was a lot of talk of drug-running operations between Spain and the United Kingdom in which Nicholas was supposed to be involved. He had somehow fallen foul of the organisation and a Mafia hit man had come to Jersey and killed him and his wife. The bodies were said to be buried at sea, or they had been put in the Bellazone incinerator, or the two had not really died at all but had just done a Lord-Lucan-type disappearing act. The police investigated each and every theory with admirable dedication, and found not a shred of evidence to support any of them. They even let a Guernsey medium, Brian Terris, conduct his own psychic investigation in the south-west part of the island where he had divined the bodies to be. Unfortunately he was 'blocked', as he put it, by the presence in the area of another body which 'wanted' to be discovered first.

Overleaf: The police burned off this headland just above Grève de Lecq, the better to search. Their efforts were in vain.

Site of the bonfire where personal effects of Elizabeth and Nicholas were found. The clearing is a little way up the cliff path from The Crows Nest.

In March 1988, the police publicly declared that they were engaged in a murder hunt. Detective Chief Superintendent John Saunders, the then head of the Suffolk CID, was called in to review the progress of the Newall investigation. Saunders had headed ten murder inquiries in Suffolk during the single year of 1987 – all of them had resulted in arrests. Coincidentally, it was at this time that Roderick Newall was on hunger strike in the Jersey prison where he was on remand on a very minor drugs charge. His action was a protest against the refusal of the police court to grant him bail. His advocate explained that Roderick Newall, now a former army officer, had used cannabis 'of late' as a form of relaxation, and to escape the pressures and sadness resulting from the disappearance of his parents, presumed murdered.

Elizabeth and Nicholas Newall's bodies have never been found. No person or persons have been charged with their murder, and this despite the most intensive, and certainly the most expensive, single murder inquiry in the history of Jersey.

What looks to be the final act was played out in the Royal Court of Jersey on Thursday 3 January 1991, 3 years after the Newalls disappeared. The *Jersey Evening Post* headline ran: 'Three Years

After the Bloodbath at Clos de L'Atlantique Court Clears the Way for the Beneficiaries to Inherit.' And, indeed, that is what the court did. Dr David Northcott said he thought the Newalls had died after an episode of sustained violence, in their own home, sometime between 10 and 18 October. He said that blood was 'sprayed' quite widely in the lounge and soaked through the carpet and underlay in the area in front of the fire. A substantial amount of blood had been found in the bedroom. The bailiff, Sir Peter Crill, did not retire but gave his verdict immediately, announcing that the court found 'that presumption (of death) was proved beyond reasonable doubt'. Thus the executors named by Elizabeth and Nicholas – the Newall brothers and Peter Barnes a barrister – could apply for the grant of probate. Mark Newall was in the court to hear this judgement; Roderick was not, for he was sailing the family yacht around the Falkland islands. The value of the Newalls' estate has not been disclosed.

And there the matter rests for the time being. The case is not closed. It cannot be closed until the killer or killers are found and that, it seems, will not happen until the bodies are discovered. Jersey is only 14.5 kilometres (9 miles) by 8 kilometres (5 miles), but there are literally thousands of places where the bodies might be concealed. As one police officer remarked, 'It's not even like finding a needle in a haystack, it's finding the haystack.' Those who remain, those who loved Elizabeth and Nicholas Newall, enjoyed their friendship and delighted in their company, may hope and pray that 'murder, though it hath no tongue will speak with most miraculous organ', if only so that they may be decently laid to rest and *finis* written to this savage, bloody and unnatural story.

BIBLIOGRAPHY

BALLEINE, G. R. *All for the king; the life story of Sir George Carteret* edit. R. Long and J. Stevens. 1976. Available from Société Jersiaise, 9 Pier Rd, St Helier, Jersey. Tel. no. 0534 58314.

BALLEINE, G. R. *History of Jersey* 2nd rev. edn. of *History of the Island of Jersey* by M. Syvret and J. Stevens. Phillimore, 1981.

BALLEINE, G. R. *Tragedy of Philippe D'Auvergne, Vice-Admiral in the Royal Navy and last Duke of Bouillon.* Phillimore, 1973.

BRETT, C. E. B. *Buildings in the town and parish of St Helier* Ulster Architectural Heritage Society, 1977, op.

BROUGH, J. *Prince and the lily* Coronet, 1978. op.

CHEVALIER, J. *Diary of Jean Chevalier* Unpublished transl. N. V. L. Rybot from original MSS, Société Jersiaise. 1643–51.

COUTANCHE, Lord *Memoires: a Jerseyman looks back* edit. H. R. S. Pocock. Phillimore, 1975.

DUDLEY, E. *Gilded Lily: the lifes and loves of the fabulous Lillie Langtry* Odhams, 1958. op.

EAGLESTON, A. J. *Channel Islands under Tudor government, 1485–1642: a study in administrative history* Cambridge U.P., 1949. op.

HYDE, E. 1st Earl of Clarendon *History of the rebellion and civil wars in England* Oxford, 1704. op.

KING, P. *Channel Islands war, 1939–45* Hale, 1991.

KIRKE, H. *From the gun room to the throne; being the life of Vice-Admiral H.S.H. Philip D'Auvergne, Duke of Bouillon* Swan Sonnenschein & Co, 1904. op.

LANGTRY, L. *Days I knew* edit. C. Lake. Redberry Press, new edn., pbk., 1989.

LEWIS, J. *Doctor's occupation* New English Library, new edn., pbk., 1980.

MAUGHAM, R. C. F. *Jersey under the jackboot* New English Library, new edn., pbk., 1980.

ONSLOW, R. *Squire: a life of George Alexander Baird gentleman rider 1861–1893* Harrap, 1980. op.

PEPYS, S. *Shorter Pepys* edit. R. Latham. Bell & Hyman, 1985; Penguin, new edn., 1987.

RYBOT, N. V. L. *Islet of St Helier and Elizabeth Castle* St Helier, 1934. op.

SINEL, L. *German occupation of Jersey: the complete diary of events from June 1940 to June 1945.* La Haule Books, 1984. op.

STEVENS, J. *Victorian voices: introduction to the papers of Sir John Le Couteur* Société Jersiaise, 1969.

VON AUFSESS, Baron *Occupation diary* Phillimore, 1985. op.

INDEX

Picture Credits

Bundesarchiv Koblenz 209
Mary Evans Picture Library 86, 102, 106, 147
German Underground Hospital Museum, Jersey 180, 181
Hulton Picture Company 33, 60, 63, 72, 74, 90, 127, 135–143, 157, 161
Jersey Evening Post 201, 221, 225, 228/229
National Maritime Museum, Greenwich 81, 85
Courtesy Michael Richecoeur 68/69
Société Jersiaise/Jersey Museum Service 2, 6, 24, 26/27, 37, 50/51, 54, 78, 97,
    100, 108, 124, 128, 137, 141, 151, 166, 170, 176, 177, 183, 185
David Ward 8–22, 30/31 34/35, 38–46, 55–58, 64/65, 92/93, 98/99, 104, 112–
    121, 131–133, 162/163, 167–169, 174/175, 178/179, 186–189.